Top Heavy, Bottom Fed

A Wake–Up Call To the Church!

By Tiffany Kameni

Dedication

I dedicate this book to my LORD and SAVIOR,
JESUS CHRIST. You are the Author and Finisher
of my faith; therefore, you are the Author of this
book. I am just Your Messenger, and I am honored
to be such.

~Tiffany Kameni

Preface

I'm not going to lie to you. There were times while writing this book that I wanted to back out because the information was so heavy-hitting that I was having trouble swallowing it. But as the LORD led me through the scriptures to back up what HE was sharing with me, I found myself feeling more relaxed, more convicted, and even more determined to make sure my life lines up with HIS WORD.

At first, I decided to write Top Heavy, Bottom Fed because of a few conversations I'd had with my husband and other believers. We would talk about politics and the church, and the information GOD was sharing to me and through me was too powerful to keep to myself.

When I started writing the book, I found myself pulling away from it again and again to go back and try to digest what I'd just found out. I can truly at this very moment say that I KNOW why GOD told us to study and show ourselves approved. There is so much that many of us don't know because we are so caught up in the day-to-day of life that we rarely stop to question if we are walking a straight and narrow line with GOD.

As I ventured further into this book, I found my reason for wanting to finish this book beginning to change. I realized that the message was not one of my own; it was coming from the Throne of Heaven. I didn't just want to finish the book anymore; I *had* to finish it! I pray this book sets you free in any area where you are bound. When you know better, you'll do better.

Introduction

Top Heavy, Bottom Fed is a powerful, dynamic book written in alarming detail about this world's system and how it affects the church.

You will never be the same after reading this book! You will learn about the American system and the principalities that rule it! You will discover why many modern-day Christian churches are practicing paganism unknowingly! Are your beliefs pagan? You will definitely find out.

Top Heavy, Bottom Fed is one of those books where you'll learn not only the present-day practices of the Christian church, but you will discover its roots! Just when you think this book couldn't get any more detailed, you will find yourself holding on to the edge of your seat as you are pulled from the depths of the lies that Satan told the church! This book is scripturally sound and backed up by the WORD!

You need a full set of teeth to read this book! Even though this book is written in a way that everyone can understand it, there is knowledge here that may be too rich for some; nevertheless, it is all backed up by scripture.

Top Heavy, Bottom Fed is a prophetic message and a warning to the church. This is a key-carrying book that was sent forth by GOD to set the prisoners free; yes, even those who are imprisoned in the church and by the doctrines that many churches have adopted.

Table of Contents

Chapter 1
Where Do You Stand?...1

Chapter 2
The World's System and the Church 9

Chapter 3
System Hierarchy...19

Chapter 4
Public Assistance or Slavery...................................41

Chapter 5
The Enemy Within..61

Chapter 6
Drugging the New Generation...............................79

Chapter 7
Chained to Debt...91

Chapter 8
The Wealth of the Wicked Is Laid Up...................113

Chapter 9
Capitalism vs. Lazarus..145

Chapter 10
Systematic Slaughter of the Church.....................165

Chapter 11
Is the Modern Church Ahab'ed?..........................177

Chapter 12
Tares Arrayed in Priestly Garments.....................195

Chapter 13
Human Branding...211

Chapter 14
Your Role Here or Your Role There......................225

Chapter 15
Principalities & Devils...235

Chapter 16
Whores of the System...265

Chapter 17
You are Not the World...279

Chapter 18
Top Heavy, Bottom Fed.......................................301

Chapter 1

<u>Where Do You Stand?</u>

Where do you stand today? What is your position in this world? What is your purpose in this world, and do you know who you are outside of the name you were given and the personality you have come to identify yourself with?

In this earth today, there are more than seven billion people in existence. Each person has his own identity, his own purpose, and his own goals. Nevertheless, the average person loses himself in the identity, plans, and goals of other souls who are either walking the earth, or have walked the earth. As people, we come into this world trying to figure out who we are, and over the course of time, we try on many identities, trying to find one that fits us the most. This signifies that we are in a process of growth and self-identification; howbeit, the average person never discovers his or her own identity because they find personalities and identities that they can fit into comfortably.

Where do you stand? Your location is where you are found at this very moment. Have you discovered who you are, or are you still letting the world's system identify you as a character type? Do you know who GOD designed you to be, or are you still trying to be someone else? Truthfully, most people could not answer this question. How can you know if you are walking in the fullness of you if you have never experienced the peace of who you really are? Of course, when we are born, we come into this world as innocent creatures, and we can only be who we are at that time. As we begin to take our first steps and develop our personalities, our first decisions to be who we are starts with our parents. Children notice that parents tend to give them more love, attention, and smiles when they act a certain way or do a certain thing. They also notice that certain behaviors and choices often go unseen; therefore, children often begin to put more emphasis on the behaviors and choices that get them more recognition. This means that as toddlers, we first started learning to drop parts of who we are to be who we believe our parents wanted us to be. As we grow up and mature, we have to go back and find the clues of who we are so that we can solve this great mystery that is our lives. By the time we became teenagers, we were so lost and confused that we likely went into a state of rebellion because our parents were telling us to

3

be who they think we should be when we wanted to find ourselves.

When we were born, sin placed us far away from GOD, and our goal was to find our way back to HIM. We were born as sinful creatures bearing the choices of our parents and their parents. We were taught to think, look, and believe a certain way to stay in our parents' good grace. When we did as we were told, our parents were often happy and peace resumed in our homes, but when we didn't do what we were told, chaos often ensued. When we became adults, we were sent out into a world full of opinions and choices. Because we were taught to care about what others thought of us, we first rebelled against the opinions of others as teens. After we became young adults, many of us tried to fit into what the collective world referred to as the norm. This means that we were lost then, but as we grew older, we became more and more lost; that is, until we decided to find our way back to CHRIST JESUS.

Many people today want to know their identities in CHRIST because they have already learned to operate under their label in the world, and they have learned to deliver what others have learned to expect from them. Daring to change could mean a loss of everything they have, because what most people have is tied in to their self-proclaimed identities!

Are you governing this world's system, or is the system governing you? Where do you stand in this man-made system, and what do you do to be your unique self? The truth is that GOD designed every individual person to be unique and stand out, but the world perceives anyone that stands out as strange. To be strange is not always a bad thing, but when we see how the world portrays people labeled as strange, the average person does not want to fit into that mold. As people of GOD, we are not supposed to involve ourselves in this world's system, because the world's system is designed to make each person a duplicate of another person. Starting in school, children are given books to read that were written by certain authors that the world's system labeled as pioneers of change. Children aren't often taught about the LORD at school because many unbelievers have fought successfully to remove prayer or any mention of JESUS CHRIST from the school system. Therefore, children are given books, studies and statistics by other human beings and told to regard them as truth. The world's idea of truth is called a fact. A fact is what has been tested and proved in the earth realm; nevertheless, a fact can be challenged and disproven. The Truth is every

Word that proceeded from the mouth of the LORD, and the <u>Truth is</u>, meaning it exists always.

GOD is peculiar, and there is no one like HIM; there has never been anyone like HIM, and there will never be anyone like HIM. The world has developed this god in their heart that agrees with their wrongs and accepts the sinful and unrepentant characters that they've learned to be. This is because they do not know the Sovereign and living GOD, JEHOVAH. Many were taught to look for HIM in religion and not in their hearts; they were taught to seek HIM with their mouths, but not with their hearts; they were taught to come to the church building, but not to understand that they are the Holy Temple of GOD. To be in HIS will is to be peculiar just like HIM. That is to be changed, renewed, and transformed into a peculiar being that carries the very glory of

GOD. We are living arks of the covenant, yet most believers have taken on the very familiar and common nature of the world that separates them from GOD.

Right now, I want you to identify your position and write it down. Draw a map of where you are and where you want to be, and record your advancement as you read this book. If you don't advance, it is only because you do not want to advance or you are expecting to be carried to a whole new understanding. The Truth will flow from this book into your heart if you are willing to receive HIM.

Chapter 2

The World's System and the Church

There were once people called the Pharisees and Sadducees. They were both religious organizations/ political presences in their day and time. The word "Pharisee" itself means "separated one." At this time, there were only Jews (GOD'S chosen people) and Gentiles, and the church was the governing body or government. The laws of the Jewish people were the Mosaic laws, and everyone that was a Jew had to follow the law to the letter.

When CHRIST walked the earth in the flesh,

HE witnessed against the common church. They'd taken on the form of a Godly institution but were really an organization set up to benefit those who were at the top, which of course were the Pharisees and Sadducees. The setup was basically what we call today a pyramid scheme. The Pharisees and Sadducees pretty much profited off of the people and enjoyed feeling empowered in their roles as governing authorities, reverencing people who were notably wealthy or renowned. Howbeit, the Pharisees and Sadducees gave off the impression that they were holy and Mosaic-law abiding priests, when in truth, they were hypocrites. This is why there were money-changers selling in the Temple. The Temple was being run as an institution of profit, and if you know the story, JESUS drove the money-changers out of the Temple with a whip. Why didn't the leaders drive the money-changers out of the Temple? Because they were benefiting from the sales that were made. This is one of the reasons that the religious leaders of that time wanted and insisted on having JESUS put to death: HE was messing with their money!

During that time, Israel was still operating under Mosaic-law, and according to the law, each family had their own land. They could sell their properties to one another if they became poor and could not afford to keep the land. Nevertheless, the nearest relative could come and redeem that land back for them, or the new owner had to release the land to the previous owner in the year of Jubilee. Jubilee occurred every fifty years. Jubilee was a GOD-instituted law that stated every slave had to be released back to their lands and families, every land had to be returned to the previous owner, and no one could sow or reap the ground during the Jubilee. It was a time of reflection and rejoicing for the people of Israel. GOD made it clear that the land was HIS own, and this law was to be carried out by the people of Israel. Initially, the law of GOD was the law of GOD'S people, and this was the official law with the Israelites.

In the book of 1 Samuel 8, you will find the story of Israel demanding a king. GOD was not pleased with their demand because HE wanted to be their King. Samuel tried to talk them out of it, but they were unrelenting. So, GOD gave them the desires of their heart. Their desiring to have a king was rooted in their desire to submit to someone other than GOD. They did not want to be led by GOD; they wanted to be led by flesh. In doing this, they were ripping the power away from the institution that GOD had set up for them, to go under a worldly system of laws and consequences.

After the death and resurrection of CHRIST JESUS, the church began to lose its governing authority as the Pharisees and Sadducees continued to battle it out for power. Christianity was demoted to just a religion instead of a lifestyle, because in Judaism, there was no religion; there was only Jew and Gentile. So, when the label "Christianity" came on the scene, it divided the Jews because many Jews did not believe upon the LORD JESUS CHRIST.

Fast forward to the era of Constantine. Constantine was the Roman Emperor from 306 to 337. Constantine was the first Roman emperor to be converted to Christianity. The Christians were being oppressed at that time, so Constantine made a law that allowed for religious tolerance. Religious tolerance was basically the right for any person to practice their own religious beliefs without the fear of retaliation. This religious tolerance was called the Edict of Milan and was signed by Constantine in 313. This law also required that any land that had been confiscated from Christians be restored to Christians.

At this time, Romans practiced paganism and wanted no part of Christianity. Most pagans worshiped a goddess they called Isis, and they wanted to continue this practice, so Constantine incorporated the idea of the Virgin Mary to replace Isis. There were many pagan beliefs incorporated into the Roman Catholic church to make Christianity more attractive to the people. The worship of Mary is called Mariology, and Mary is noted as the "Queen of Heaven" just as the pagans had originally referred to Isis. At this time, most Europeans were Celts and held certain ritualistic practices such as annual Halloween celebrations. Again, the Catholic church welcomed these beliefs because they wanted to transition the people from paganism to Christianity with as little resistance as possible.

The Roman Catholic Church had a hierarchy established, with the Pope being regarded as the highest ranking person in the religion. Under the Pope was the Cardinals, Archbishops, Bishops, Priests, and finally the Monks and Nuns. As noted earlier, there were certain practices that were native to the Celts and other pagans that were allowed into the Catholic church for the sole purpose of getting the approval of the people. This was the start of what would one day be known as a government for the people and by the people.

Roman Catholicism made its way to Europe by the first century, as stated earlier, having been brought in first by Constantine. It took between 300 to 400 years before England became

Christianized. Even after its conversion, England and much of Europe retained many of its Celtic traditions.

Let's fast forward again. By the 1500s, the kings in Europe were the governing authorities; however, the Catholic church was just as, if not more, powerful. The king was subject to the laws of the church. At this time, the government and the church worked together; whereas in earlier times, the church was the governing authority. In 1509, Henry VIII became King of England by default. His brother Arthur should have become king, but he died, making King Henry the successor. In accordance with Old Testament law, the king inherited his brother's wife and was supposed to raise kids up in the name of his brother. Nevertheless, King Henry's wife, Catherine of Aragon, had a daughter instead of a son. At this time, men did not know that the gender of the child depended solely upon their (the man's) chromosomes. It was widely believed that the woman determined the gender of the child. Because the child was a girl, Henry petitioned the Pope to give him a divorce because his wife did not conceive a son for him. Since his desire for a divorce was biblically unsound, the Pope would not grant him his request; therefore, the king appointed a new Archbishop called Thomas Cramer. This angered the Pope, who then excommunicated King Henry. To be excommunicated was an extremely bad thing, and it meant that your membership to that religion was terminated or suspended until further notice. Because of this, King Henry stripped the church of its power and declared himself as the leader of the church. This act was called the Act of Supremacy. If you know the story, King Henry went on to be married a total of six times, having had two of his wives executed. The Act

17

of Supremacy was the start of the repositioning of the church, whereas the church was no longer revered as the governing authority but was then made subject to the king.

Then came the divine right of kings doctrine, which was brought to England by James I of England in 1603. The divine right of kings basically states that the monarch (king or queen) is subject only to GOD and is not subject to any earthly authority. This doctrine was abandoned by England in 1688, and by the early twentieth century, it had been abandoned totally by Europe and America. This doctrine established the king as the absolute authority over the people and basically told them that they could not question his acts or decisions, but that he could only be judged by GOD. It was believed that the Pope had spiritual authority, and the king had earthly authority.

Chapter 3

System Hierarchy

The British government went through many changes over the years because of the much expected power struggles that arose from within government.

Feudalism:

1. A political and economic system of Europe from the 9th to about the 15th century, based on the holding of all land in fief or fee and the resulting relation of lord to vassal and characterized by homage, legal and military service of tenants, and forfeiture.

2. A political, economic, or social order

resembling this medieval system.

Reference: The Free Dictionary

Feudalism was a set of legal and military customs in medieval Europe that flourished between the 9th and 15th centuries, which, broadly defined, was a system for structuring society around relationships derived from the holding of land in exchange for service or labor.

Reference: Wikipedia

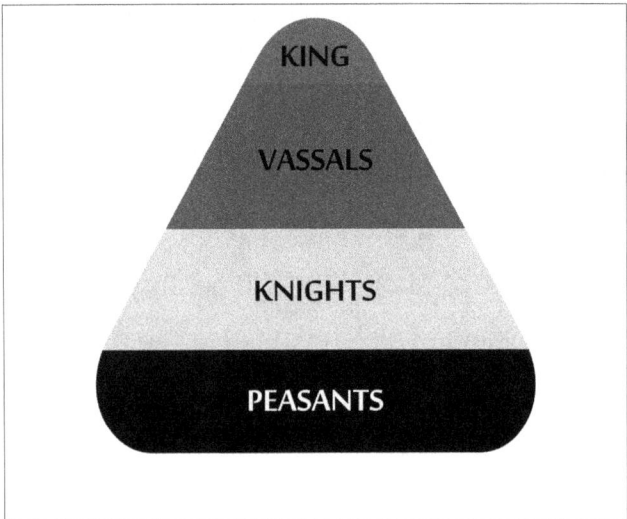

As you can see from the chart above, the king was the ultimate authority, and he was paid homage by the nobles. The nobles were noblemen that included: Lords, Barons, Bishops, Earls, and Abbots. The king owned all the land, and he allowed the nobles to stay on the land in exchange for their servitude. The nobles would fight for the king whenever he commanded, and the king would protect the nobles from any external forces. The nobles would also pay taxes to the king and provide knights for the king.

The nobles would become lords over knights. The nobles would portion out some of the land the king gave to them to their knights and commit to protecting the knights and their families from external forces. In exchange, the knights would provide them military protection and servitude.

Finally, there were the peasants. The peasants were the general workers who were given land by the knights in exchange for labor, farming, money, and military service. Peasants could be broken up into three categories: freeman, serf, or slave.

As you can see, the world's system then was setup to benefit the person at the top of the pyramid the most, and that person was the king. The nobles were considered prestigious because they fell directly under the king and were given titles, rank, and power by the king.

Feudalism reached its peak in the 13th to 14th centuries and was replaced by the Renaissance in the 15th century. But did feudalism truly end? If you look at the setup of today's system, you will see that feudalism is very much alive; however, there were more tiers added to the pyramid, and throughout the years, roles have been redefined again and again to benefit those who are at the top of the pyramid.

In a feudalistic government, it was almost impossible for a peasant or a peasant's children to move up the pyramid of rank. If your father was a farmer, you would likely be a farmer along with your siblings. In addition, to marry someone beneath your rank was frowned upon.

Today, we have replaced feudalism with capitalism. Capitalism is *"an economic system in which investment in and ownership of the means of production, distribution, and exchange of wealth is made and maintained chiefly by private individuals or corporations." (Reference: The Free Dictionary)* Capitalism allows for the rise of the poor, and the fall of the great; nevertheless in a

23

capitalistic government, those who have rank rarely fall because of the pyramid structure. They are held up by the servants that are underneath them, but it is not impossible for them to fall; howbeit rare.

With capitalism, power still rests in the hands of those that are at the top of the pyramid, but a modern-day peasant could rise up to become a noble if he or she earned or inherited the money to do so. Instead of ranking by title, in a capitalistic nation, one is ranked high by what he has or low by what he doesn't have.

Nowadays, as American citizens, we live in what is called a democratic government. Abraham Lincoln said this of democracy: *"A government of the people, by the people, for the people, shall not perish from the Earth."* We are taught that democracy means that the power is no longer at the top of the pyramid but in the hands of the people. The U.S. President is not a dictator and does not possess absolute power but instead is given the appearance of power without the presence of power. According to the United States Constitution, the power is in the hands of the people. Let me share with you why this is wrong on so many levels. First off, GOD appointed kings to rule HIS people. These kings would either be righteous and cause the land and the people to be blessed, or they would be unrighteous and cause the land and the people to sin against GOD. These kings would rule until their deaths. A righteous king ruled by the law of GOD and judged GOD'S people accordingly. Of course, the President in our system is our version of a king. The problem with the people being in the ruling seat is that all you need is a large number of sinners to come out and protest GOD'S WORD, and our government will make a law that goes against GOD'S

WORD. This is because the people who actually make the laws want to please the people and get re-elected; therefore, we become a dark nation who wears the appearance of power without the presence of power. It goes without saying that America has become a nation of wickedness, and the righteous are becoming fewer and fewer as the people battle for the right to sin against GOD.

Should the rights of the people be taken away? Should man be forced to live by a book that many don't even believe in? After all, GOD doesn't take away our rights to make choices. In the Bible, you will find that the Gentiles were a nation of wicked people, just as the Jews were a righteous nation (when they were acting right). Therefore, people have the right to be as wicked as they want to be; **however**, they were separated, and the darkness (wicked people) could not dwell amongst the light

(GOD'S people) because sinners often cause the righteous to fall, as witnessed daily in our nation. So what you are witnessing is the actual mixing of the tares and the wheat as mentioned in Matthew 13:24-30. *"Another parable put he forth unto them, saying, The kingdom of heaven is likened unto a man which sowed good seed in his field: But while men slept, his enemy came and sowed tares among the wheat, and went his way. But when the blade was sprung up, and brought forth fruit, then appeared the tares also. So the servants of the householder came and said unto him, Sir, didst not thou sow good seed in thy field? From whence then hath it tares? He said unto them, An enemy hath done this. The servants said unto him, Wilt thou then that we go and gather them up? But he said, Nay; lest while ye gather up the tares, ye root up also the wheat with them. Let both grow together until the harvest: and in the time of harvest I*

will say to the reapers, Gather ye together first
the tares, and bind them in bundles to burn
them: but gather the wheat into my barn."

When asked about the meaning of the parable,
JESUS spoke this:

"Then Jesus sent the multitude away, and went
into the house: and his disciples came unto
him, saying, Declare unto us the parable of the
tares of the field. He answered and said unto
them, He that soweth the good seed is the Son
of man; The field is the world; the good seed
are the children of the kingdom; but the tares
are the children of the wicked one; The enemy
that sowed them is the devil; the harvest is the
end of the world; and the reapers are the
angels. As therefore the tares are gathered
and burned in the fire; so shall it be in the end
of this world. The Son of man shall send forth
his angels, and they shall gather out of his
kingdom all things that offend, and them which

do iniquity; And shall cast them into a furnace of fire: there shall be wailing and gnashing of teeth. Then shall the righteous shine forth as the sun in the kingdom of their Father. Who hath ears to hear, let him hear" (Matthew *13:36-43).* (Note: If you have trouble understanding the King James version above, review the scriptures in the NIV version).

Nevertheless, the people of GOD have to separate themselves from the world and the world's system or be forced to submit to the world's system by the tares that run it. How does one separate himself? Simply by reading, hearing, knowing and applying the WORD of GOD and not submitting to the system of this world when it seems beneficial to them. This means that you should by no means go under the world's system, because the world's system is set up to water the tares and destroy the wheat. The system of this world is designed to make the people feel as if they have the power, but in truth, they don't. Just like the President doesn't have absolute power, the people have limited power. Where does this power rest? In the hands of the elected officials who control your tax dollars. Read Section 8 of the United States Constitution below:

"1: The Congress shall have Power To lay and collect Taxes, Duties, Imposts and Excises, to pay the Debts and provide for the common Defence and general Welfare of the United States; but all Duties, Imposts and Excises shall be uniform throughout the United States;

2: To borrow Money on the credit of the United States;

3: To regulate Commerce with foreign Nations, and among the several States, and with the Indian Tribes;

4: To establish an uniform Rule of Naturalization, and uniform Laws on the subject of Bankruptcies throughout the United

States;

5: To coin Money, regulate the Value thereof, and of foreign Coin, and fix the Standard of Weights and Measures;

6: To provide for the Punishment of counterfeiting the Securities and current Coin of the United States;

7. To establish Post Offices and post Roads;

8: To promote the Progress of Science and useful Arts, by securing for limited Times to Authors and Inventors the exclusive Right to their respective Writings and Discoveries;

9: To constitute Tribunals inferior to the supreme Court;

10: To define and punish Piracies and Felonies committed on the high Seas, and Offences against the Law of Nations;

11: To declare War, grant Letters of Marque and Reprisal, and make Rules concerning

Captures on Land and Water;

12: To raise and support Armies, but no Appropriation of Money to that Use shall be for a longer Term than two Years;

13: To provide and maintain a Navy;

14: To make Rules for the Government and Regulation of the land and naval Forces;

15: To provide for calling forth the Militia to execute the Laws of the Union, suppress Insurrections and repel Invasions;

16: To provide for organizing, arming, and disciplining, the Militia, and for governing such Part of them as may be employed in the Service of the United States, reserving to the States respectively, the Appointment of the Officers, and the Authority of training the Militia according to the discipline prescribed by Congress;

17: To exercise exclusive Legislation in all Cases whatsoever, over such District (not exceeding ten Miles square) as may, by Cession of particular States, and the Acceptance of Congress, become the Seat of the Government of the United States, and to exercise like Authority over all Places purchased by the Consent of the Legislature of the State in which the Same shall be, for the Erection of Forts, Magazines, Arsenals, dock-Yards, and other needful Buildings;--And

18: To make all Laws which shall be necessary and proper for carrying into Execution the foregoing Powers, and all other Powers vested by this Constitution in the Government of the United States, or in any Department or Officer thereof."

As you can see, the power is not in the hands of the people. At the same time, in any GOD-ordained institution, the people are not supposed to have the power: GOD is! GOD positions righteous men to lead HIS people, but when you go under a system that is set up for the people, you are under a capitalistic system who cares more about earning your dollars than the salvation of your soul. *"When the righteous are in authority, the people rejoice: but when the wicked beareth rule, the people mourn" (Joshua 29:2).* The power is not in the hands of the President, and thankfully so, because the President is chosen by the people and controlled by the Congress.

A PRESIDENT CAN.......................................

- make treaties <u>with the approval of the Senate</u>.

- veto bills and sign bills.

- represent our nation in <u>talks</u> with foreign countries.

- enforce the laws that <u>Congress passes</u>.

- <u>act</u> as Commander-in-Chief during a war.

- <u>call</u> out troops to protect our nation against an attack.

- <u>make suggestions</u> about things that should be new laws.

- <u>lead his</u> political party.

- <u>entertain</u> foreign guests.

- <u>recognize</u> foreign countries.

- grant pardons.

- <u>nominate</u> Cabinet members and Supreme Court Justices and other high officials.

- appoint ambassadors.

- <u>talk</u> directly to the people about problems.

- <u>represent</u> the best interest of all the people.

A PRESIDENT CANNOT................................

- make laws.

- declare war.

- decide how federal money will be spent.

- interpret laws.

- choose Cabinet members or Supreme Court Justices without Senate approval."

(Reference: Harry Truman)

So basically, the President can't do much without the approval of the Senate; he can talk, nominate, represent, call, recognize, entertain, lead his political party, and make suggestions. It's actually pretty sad how the American people are revved up to make such a big deal about a Presidential election when the real power rests in the hands of Congress. (Note to the church: If you really want to affect change, don't put so much stock into the Presidential election; put stock into those that are pulling his strings). *"For we wrestle not against flesh and blood, but against principalities, against powers, against the rulers of the darkness of this world, against spiritual wickedness in high places" (Ephesians 6:12).*

We live in a nation where the President is more esteemed than the Almighty GOD but has little to no power. We live in a nation where the Bible was replaced by the U.S. Constitution, and a man can be punished for violating the Constitution, but he is free to go against the WORD of GOD. (As a believer, if you have never believed that the world's system is against you, you were sideswiped and blinded by a system that was "nice enough" to cover your eyes while it raped and plundered you). We live in a nation where prayer is no longer allowed in school, but a pagan holiday (Halloween) is, and the Constitution is taught to our children without fail. We live in a nation where the rights of the criminal surpass the rights of the victim. We live in a nation where it is illegal to burn the American flag (America's idol), but you can burn a Bible without fear of consequence. We live in a powerful nation, but what kind of powers are in operation here?

The top of the American system is Congress, and many Congressmen are often the puppets of the people who fund their campaigns. Money is what drives the United States government, and just like any pyramid scheme, the people at the bottom of the triangle are the ones who pay the most but work the hardest to hold up the people at the top. Where do you stand in this hierarchy? If you are a believer, you shouldn't be standing in it at all. Believers nowadays involve themselves so much into this government and its setup and even condemn other believers who simply try to live their lives by the WORD of GOD. *"Ye adulterers and adulteresses, know ye not that the friendship of the world is enmity with God? Whosoever therefore will be a friend of the world is the enemy of God" (James 4:4).*

Just know that as a believer, if you link yourself up to this wicked system, you will be considered the least of the system, and as such, you will be required to hold up their erected idols. This includes the mighty dollar. CHRIST is above the world's system, and everyone who is in HIM is above it. Everyone who is involved with the system of this world is under the law of this world. *"Far above all principality, and power, and might, and dominion, and every name that is named, not only in this age, but also in that which is to come: And has put all things under his feet, and gave him to be the head over all things to the church, Which is his body, the fullness of him that fills all in all" (Ephesians 1:21-23).*

Chapter 4

<u>Public Assistance or Slavery</u>

You'd be amazed at the structure of the American economic system and many Western systems. In the days of old, a man was prohibited from crossing over the lines of being a peasant to being a noble in the British system. This line was crossed less than a handful of times because this British system was designed to keep the poor poor and to help the wealthy get wealthier. Nowadays, the poor can cross over to become someone great, but the system discourages the crossing over by supplying any man under it with barely enough to survive and then pulling the plug on his assistance should he dare try to do better.

There are many people who get welfare and social security checks. Many are slaves of this worldly system and cannot fathom losing their assistance. I have witnessed how people who are accustomed to getting financial assistance are cut off when they decide to get a job or try to improve their lives. Because of this, they had to go back under a system that chained them to lack and told them to stay there. Understand that many people who are on welfare are college educated; nevertheless, many of the jobs they are offered will only pay them less than or equal to what they are getting in their monthly assistance checks! For the ones who are offered more, the difference in what's offered to them isn't a big difference from what they get in their checks, and then they still have taxes to look forward to. So if you are sitting at home and getting paid to do so, you're likely not going to go to work to get the same amount of money you could have gotten sitting at home. Getting a job is actually discouraged unless the welfare recipient applies for a part-time job that doesn't pay them too much. You would probably ask why the government discourages people from getting full-time jobs and possibly relieve the system of the billions of dollars it pays out in public assistance. It goes back to the system of hierarchy. People who are poor often create poor children who grow up to labor for the children of the people who are rich. After all, you can't teach a child more than you know. There are many who will argue that the American system gives college grants to many who want to "cross over." That's because the system is capitalistic. There are many geniuses living in poverty-stricken areas, and the government only welcomes this crossing over when it benefits their system. There are many requirements that prohibit many from getting those grants. You will need an average grade G.P.A. of 2.0 to be eligible for a grant. Nevertheless, the crossing over isn't a peasant (as labeled by the original system) becoming a noble; the crossing over is a peasant becoming a middle-class citizen. Why is that? Because the middle-class is the heart of the American system. The rich does not fund public assistance; the middle-class does!

There are three ranking systems recognized by the American people, and they are upper-class, middle-class, and lower-class. The top 1% of Americans (the rich) own **40%** of the nations wealth! So even though the top of the pyramid is extremely narrow and pointy, its assets are robust. Even within the ranking system, there are still levels. For example, you may have heard the terms "upper middle-class" and "lower middle-class". This identifies the subjects by their income.

More than half of Americans do not pay income tax, and this has angered the wealthy. The wealthy claim that it is unfair that they are taxed so heftily while the lower-class are not. This was made public when Mitt Romney gave his famous "47%" speech, claiming that 47% of Americans who did not pay taxes would vote for President Obama. But the truth of the matter is the middle-class are the ones who hold up the bulk of the load. The American system gives the tax dollars back to the laborers because the laborers are the system's foundation, and the upper middle-class are like the knights of the system. Each class is like a tier that benefits the class directly above it and is supported by the class directly below it. So even when the wealthy are paying taxes, they are, in reality, simply being forced to give back some of the money that they have earned off the people at the bottom of the totem pole. *(And in truth, the wealthy often pay a lower tax percentage than the less fortunate).* The average company may earn more than one thousand dollars a day off of one individual worker, but still only pay that worker $7 per hour. Multiply that by 8 hours, and the worker is earning $56 a day. Needless to say, the average company is earning $7,000 a week per person and paying those individuals $280 week! In an attempt to keep their money, many millionaires often close branches of their companies when they are forced to pay out more money, even though they would still be getting the bulk of it. Many times this is done to cripple the American system by causing the many middle-class citizens and lower-class citizens to be out of work. No work means less tax dollars the United States government can get from the middle-class, and it also means more pressure the middle-class and lower middle-class will put on the elected officials. In other words, many wealthy people have learned to use the people as weapons against themselves for their own personal advancement.

Do you recall the story about the rich man and Lazarus, the beggar? *"There was a certain rich man, which was clothed in purple and fine linen, and fared sumptuously every day: And there was a certain beggar named Lazarus, which was laid at his gate, full of sores, And desiring to be fed with the crumbs which fell from the rich man's table: moreover the dogs came and licked his sores" (Luke 16:19-21).* In this story, you can see that the rich man lived in luxury and without need, but poor Lazarus desired to at least eat the crumbs that fell from the rich man's table. If you continue the story, you will find that the rich man basically ignored Lazarus, yet he knew Lazarus's name. This means he understood that Lazarus had a want and a need, but the rich man was more concerned about living in luxury than he was about even helping Lazarus to stay alive. How do we know he knew Lazarus's name? The scriptures tell us that when he went to hell, he asked Abraham to let Lazarus bring him a drop of water. He didn't ask Abraham to give him any water; he asked Abraham to get Lazarus to do it. This tells us that even in hell, he felt that he outranked Lazarus, but Abraham had to set the record straight. After this, he still asked Abraham to send Lazarus to warn his family. What's the point of the story? There are many people in the world's system who are hungry, and they would do anything to get the crumbs that fall from the tables of the 1% who own 40% of all the nation's wealth. There are many who are covered in sores, or without healthcare, who sit at the gate of the wealthy, hoping to be seen and cared for. But most wealthy people care more about keeping what they have and getting wealthier than they do about the lives of the people who are sustaining their lifestyles.

Why would you, as a believer, want to be a part of a system that continues to ignore its Lazarus? How many believers have to lift up their eyes in hell before they realize that anyone that is a friend of the world is an enemy of GOD?

What if you are a part of this worldly system? You are getting public assistance, and you have learned how to master being poor? Chances are you will teach this to your children, and they will teach it to their children, and the feudal system will continue to live on

49

under a different name. What you may not realize is that you are a peasant who helps to balance the 1% at the top of the pyramid. What is being given to you has been taken from someone else. It's not taken from the 1%, but it is taken from the middle-class. You are being encouraged to stay in crime-ridden areas. In fact, the government will often pay your rent over there, and you will move around from house to house all of your life. In other words, you will become a vagabond.

Wikipedia defines a vagabond this way: *"A vagrant or a vagabond is a person, often in poverty, who wanders from place to place without a home or regular employment or income. Other synonyms include "tramp", "hobo", and "drifter", all of which have pejorative connotations. A vagrant is "a person without a settled home or regular work who wanders from place to place and lives by begging;" vagrancy is the condition of such persons." (Reference: Wikipedia).*

We were taught that a vagabond or hobo was a person who lived on the street and had no physical address, but this isn't true. A vagabond is anyone who does not have a regular home, employment or income.

As Americans, we are all vagabonds through the American system. How is that? Even if you buy a home in the United States of America, you will never own that home. If you don't believe me, stop paying your property taxes and see what happens. You simply pay for the right to call it yours. In the United States, to buy a home is to simply purchase it from the last person or business who was basically renting it from our government. After you start buying that home, you are given information on how and where to pay your property taxes. If you do not pay property taxes, your house will be auctioned off or foreclosed on. Should you "buy" a home? Absolutely, because you're going to pay the government taxes either way to live under its system. The government basically promises to provide you protection against outside forces in exchange for your labor.

Most Americans are unsettled vagabonds because we move simultaneously with our finances. When our finances aren't looking so well, we settle into a place we feel we can afford. When our finances are looking up, we move up into a place we feel we deserve.

When the economy is down, many homeowners become renters because they are often laid off from their jobs. The world's system is designed to keep the man at the top from falling. The middle-class is a cushion for the upper-crust. Those at the top often suffer what I can best describe as a mosquito bite when the economy fails. How so? Imagine if you had ten thousand dollars and you gave one dollar to ten workers every day. Each worker earned a thousand dollars for you daily. Suddenly your supplier has to go up on his supplies for whatever reason. To compensate for that, you now have to either raise the price of the products and services you offer, or you have to lay off some of your workers. Let's say you were paying your supplier $10 per box of tissue, but now the supplier is charging $12 per box. Now, you'll still be wealthy if you left things as they were, but you would lose an extra $2 in profit. This wasn't your goal, however. Your plan was to expand your company, and you've actually invested into some new fixtures for the expansion. Again, there is a work-around here. You could easily put those fixtures aside and plan to expand later, but you choose to let some of your workers go so you won't be hit as hard financially. Keep in mind that you are wealthy, and you can afford the hit; it's just an inconvenience to you because even millionaires want to get richer.

Again, what ends up happening is people lose their jobs, homes and their security so that the rich won't end up having to compromise their luxurious lifestyles. As a matter of fact, some wealthy people reportedly got wealthier during the recession. On the other hand, most people on or beneath the poverty line live their lives in transition. They move from one place to the next because many search for homes that will allow them more money to pay their bills, while some do it to have more spending money. With the majority of Americans being lower middle-class to poor, what keeps the people from coming together as one against a system that uses them as end tables for the wealthy? The answer is simple. In a lot of our prisons, there is only one guard per five inmates. The inmates are strong enough to take the prison; that goes without saying, but the prison learns to isolate people who could and would cause such an uproar. Let's face it; most people in prison are extreme followers; that's why they are in prison. Without a leader, a follower will follow the rules out of fear. The point here is Americans are the same way. The top earners are the one percent, and they control the wealth of the entire nation! Most Americans are followers who stay in place because they fear being a thumb; most people are comfortable being fingers. The thumb stands out and is expected to place a firm grip of whatever it attempts to carry. The thumb is the strongest finger on the human hand; therefore, anyone who stands out has to be strong and knowledgeable before they can grip the minds and attention of a people who are accustomed to being fingers.

When you depend on the government for assistance, you are in the same bound by the government, its practices and its laws. When you depend on the government, you are a slave to the system of this world, and you must follow the rules in order to have a place to lay your head, a job and a vehicle. The American system has quickly became an enemy to GOD because it enslaves the people under it. America was once a country that boasted on freedom for its people; nowadays, it's a country that has been ensnared by a spirit of greed. America makes slaves out of its inhabitants for shear gain. GOD set us free with HIS SON; therefore, to go back into bondage is senseless. *"If the Son therefore shall make you free, ye shall be free indeed" (John 8:36).* The system hasn't changed much; it simply changed what it told the people serving under it.

But what if you need welfare? Are you a slave to the system, and should you deny yourself the benefits since you are a believer? No way. If you need the benefits, get them. The welfare program can be good if you use it as a means of help while you are in transition. For example, if you lost your job or if your job was to cut down your hours, you should tap into the welfare program to get some of that money out that they have taken from you over the years. After all, that was the purpose of the program. It was supposed to be used by people who could not work because of physical limitations and to help those who are between jobs or not earning enough to feed their families. All the same, think of it as a temporary parking place where you have paid the meter to let you park there for a set amount of time. Always set out to do what it is you were called by GOD to do so you can move your vehicle. Understand that GOD never intended for HIS people to be in lack. Believers often fall under lack when they have learned to lean on the system of this world. The folding of the system does not always represent an attack from the enemy; sometimes, the loss of a job or the uncertainty you have at work bears witness to the fact that you can only rely on GOD.

As Christians, you should be developing strategies to start your own businesses. You should be tapping into your GOD-given gifts and talents. After all, the world trains those in it according to another man's knowledge. But you are a peculiar people, and you should never allow yourselves to become a Lazarus to the system. After all, you belong to GOD and should not be ruled by man! *"The rich ruleth over the poor, and the borrower is servant to the lender" (Proverbs 22:7)*. Don't let fear keep you from standing on the promises of GOD, for the WORD of GOD is a foundation that will never give away from under you. Any time the world is feeding the believer, something is wrong! The world is supposed to be coming to us, and not the other way around! *"The LORD will make you the head, not the tail. If you pay attention to the commands of the LORD your God that I give you this day and carefully follow them, you will always be at the top, never at the bottom" (Deuteronomy 28:13 NIV).*

Chapter 5

The Enemy Within

As you know, our country has a problem with obesity. A lot of our foods are either processed, full of hormones, full of sugar, or full of artificial ingredients that the body has trouble digesting. These foods taste great and many have been reported to be addictive; however, they work against our bodies, not for them. Our body is able to extract a minimum amount of nutrients from some of these foods, but in many cases, there are no nutrients to be absorbed. We are a nation of people who have learned to feed our hunger pains and ignore our health.

Many of the companies that produce these foods are fully aware that the foods are dangerous, but they continue making them because they want your money. After all, most people don't question what goes into their bodies because they tend to trust that any food that made it past the FDA must be safe. This is just not true. The FDA has approved and then recalled many food and drug brands after the human testing period was over. What does "the human testing period" mean? What happens is the companies don't do a lot of research on the effects of what they will be selling. The FDA does not check these foods; they pull them only after they have been reported to cause illness or death. USA Today spoke to Gregory Jaffe, and one of their questions to him was: **Does the FDA test these foods before they're allowed on the**

market? *(By "these" foods they meant genetically manufactured foods).* Gregory's answer to this question was: *"No. Instead, there is a voluntary consultation process. Genetically engineered foods are overseen by the FDA, but there is no approval process. Foods are presumed to be safe unless the FDA has evidence to the contrary, Jaffe says. The FDA "has to show that there may be a problem with the food, as opposed to the company needing to prove it's safe to FDA's satisfaction before it can get on the market," he says."*

Again, the goal is to make money; that's it, and there is no other motive. Foods are manufactured to fatten up the pockets of the upper-crust; at the same time, those who eat it are fattened, and their life expectancy decreases.

When food enters your body, it will nourish it, ignore it, or attack it. It's amazing how much damage a cheeseburger can do. Once you start to eat processed foods and anything unhealthy for you, you will likely develop a craving or lust for that particular food. Every time you indulge yourself, you invite another attack to your body. The chemicals in many of the foods we eat have been proven to be associated with cancer. That's why food can sometimes become "the enemy within." Something as small as a mouth can open up big enough to swallow death whole.

America does the same with its people. This country is being poisoned from within by greed. One percent of Americans have the power to determine what the others eat, how they live and how their earnings will be distributed. Because of this, poverty has gripped America, and crime is going up by the day. You have to understand that, by nurturing a small percentage of its people and ignoring (sometimes starving) the majority of its people, America is now like that mouth. Greed is swallowed whole and births a deadly mindset in those who are barely getting by. We all say that most of the criminals need to get an education and a job; and this is true! Howbeit, there are many small people with big dreams, and they won't settle for lower or lower middle-class. All the same, the American system pumps more money into opening and financing more prisons than it does into opening and financing more schools. This tells you about the direction we are headed in. Many who are at the top are trying to find ways to contain those who are at the bottom. There isn't much thought put into advancing the next generation; after all, this is a capitalistic nation whose focus is on more, more and more. Because of this, most Americans have developed a tribal mindset; that is, they stick to people who are like-minded. Poor people stick to others who can relate to them, wealthy people stick to wealthy people, and each race tends to stick to its own. Division is the first split in a country before it collapses.

Tribalism:
1. The organization, culture, or beliefs of a tribe.
2. A strong feeling of identity with and loyalty to one's tribe or group.
Reference: The Free Dictionary

Tribalism is the state of being organized in, or advocating for, a tribe or tribes. In terms of conformity, tribalism may also refer to a way of thinking or behaving in which people are more loyal to their tribe than to their friends, their country, or any other social group.
Reference: Wikipedia

Do you remember when Mitt Romney referred to the 47% of Americans who he said would vote for Obama? These were the people who allegedly didn't pay income taxes. Why was his comment so widely rebuked? It's simple: as a divided country, we are not allowed to speak against someone in a group other than our own. For example, as an African American, I can easily rebuke my race for something that I see out of place; nevertheless, a Caucasian American could not do this. If I were to criticize a Caucasian American for something I felt was common to the race, my rebuke would not be met with laughter because I am not Caucasian. The point is, we are a people who consider it immoral for someone unlike us to speak against us. If the rebuke comes from within, we see it as a correction or an observation; if the rebuke comes from the outside, we see it as judgment. This mindset bears witness to a divide in America that keeps swallowing the opportunity for growth whole. Any time you see division, you are witnessing the domino effect to destruction. There are all types of divides in America; some positive and some negative. Because of this, many Americans are against their neighbors, since their neighbors are different from them. I remember some years ago, when I was married to my first husband, we'd moved into this wealthy neighborhood. Where we lived, there were mostly doctors, lawyers and politicians. We were the only blacks on that street. What I noticed was none of the neighbors came over to greet us when we'd moved in. Some of them wouldn't even greet us if they saw us standing outside. One of our neighbors ended up losing his house to foreclosure, and another couple came along and purchased it a few months later. They were a Caucasian couple, and even though they were kind of stand-offish, they were friendly whenever we saw them outside. One day, we happened to notice a lot of people at their home, and we were told it was a welcoming party. Some of the people of the neighborhood came there to welcome them to the neighborhood. We joked that no one had come out to welcome us, but they were throwing a party for our neighbors. We weren't offended too much because we understood that people tend to stick around who they feel they can relate to the most. All the same, people tend to fear and ostracize people who are not like them. This type of mentality causes division.

These are the types of mindsets that America breeds. One of the mottos used in America was coined in 1942 by John Dickinson. It came from a song he'd written called *The Liberty Song*. Was this statement prophetic in nature? The statement is: *United we stand;*

divided we fall. How true is this? It bears witness to what GOD said when the people were building a tower to Heaven in Genesis 11:6. *"And the LORD said, Behold, the people are one, and they have all one language; and this they begin to do: and now nothing will be restrained from them, which they have imagined to do."*

This is a country of tribalism where there are divides in divided groups! For example, there are rich racists and there are poor racists. The rich racists don't ordinarily associate with the poor ones, because the poor have nothing to lose and therefore may prove to be more of a liability. GOD designed us to unite, but Satan corrupted us to divide so that he could conquer us. There is so much power in unity, but America will likely never embrace this love or power because of its love of money and lack of knowledge. Because of this, the American system has created an enemy within. So many militant and terrorist groups are terrorizing this country for various reasons. People are going into schools and public buildings, shooting and killing random people for no apparent reason. That's because this country encourages the "every man for himself" mindset, and this is **absolutely dangerous**. Selfishness is what got Satan evicted from Heaven, and selfishness is a man's attempt to establish his identity as a god. If he gets the chance to feel glorified through a few moments of terror, he will embrace the opportunity because selfishness has twisted his mind; division has strangled his conscious, and instability has given him a sense of purpose. One selfish man can be a danger to thousands of divided people. Of course, the only divide GOD welcomes is the divide of the believer from the unbeliever.

Where does this selfishness come from? Everything we stand on has a foundation and a roof. With America, for the most part, you are dealing with worldly politicians who have no real relationship with GOD. Many know HIS Name and even attend church services regularly, but their fruit bears witness to whom they serve. Their foundation is the lusts of this world, and they have become the rooftops for many people who trust them to pass laws to make their lives better. Many Americans trust them to distribute the wealth; instead, they consume it upon their own lusts. The selfishness on these people trickles on down, and a lot of people (followers) who desire to be in the top ranks of American society do desperate things to get there. They know the wealth isn't distributed fairly, and they know that they'll likely never get there legally; therefore, many people resort to a life of crime. Their love of money and lack of knowledge makes them just like the politicians and wealth-mongers who don't think about the lives that will be lost or ruined to get and maintain them in the lifestyle they want. This is why GOD discourages selfishness. This is why HE told the church to not forsake the coming together of the saints. GOD wants us to see that others are struggling just as we are, so we won't get so entangled in self-pity to the point where we become self-righteous, self-centered and self-absorbed.

When the people share in the wealth, knowledge and understanding, everyone will become wealthy. The problem is a spirit called greed. This is when a person is not content with being wealthy; he wants more, no matter what the costs are. There was a time in the Bible when the people of GOD came together and shared the wealth. Acts 4:32-35 tells us about this time: *All the believers were one in heart and mind. No one claimed that any of their possessions was their own, but they shared everything they had. With great power the apostles continued to testify to the resurrection of the Lord Jesus. And God's grace was so powerfully at work in them all that there were no needy persons among them. For from time to time those who owned land or houses sold them, brought the money from the sales and put it at the apostles' feet, and it was distributed to anyone who had need.*

This was a time of GOD'S glory indeed. In sharing the wealth, the people were being taught to be selfless, not selfish. This undoubtedly is the act of love that invites the presence of GOD. Then, here came Ananias with his selfish mindset. Even though he had more than enough, he didn't want to share his wealth; nevertheless, I'm sure he didn't have a problem reaching into what was being distributed. Acts 5:1-11 elaborates more on this story: *Now a man named Ananias, together with his wife Sapphira, also sold a piece of property. With his wife's full knowledge he kept back part of the money for himself, but brought the rest and put it at the apostles' feet.*

Then Peter said, "Ananias, how is it that Satan has so filled your heart that you have lied to the Holy Spirit and have kept for yourself some of the money you received for the land? Didn't it belong to you before it was sold? And after it was sold, wasn't the money at your disposal? What made you think of doing such a thing? You have not lied just to human beings but to God."

When Ananias heard this, he fell down and died. And great fear seized all who heard what had happened. Then some young men came forward, wrapped up his body, and carried him out and buried him.

About three hours later his wife came in, not knowing what had happened. Peter asked her, "Tell me, is this the price you and Ananias got for the land?"

"Yes," she said, "that is the price."

Peter said to her, "How could you conspire to test the Spirit of the Lord? Listen! The feet of the men who buried your husband are at the door, and they will carry you out also."

At that moment she fell down at his feet and died. Then the young men came in and, finding her dead, carried her out and buried her beside her husband. Great fear seized the whole church and all who heard about these events.

GOD knew that Ananias and his wife would be an enemy to the people. They would be a poison that promoted selfishness rather than unity. They would be the instruments Satan utilized to destroy what GOD had used HIS Apostles to bring together. They would become the enemies from within.

In order to reduce crime, selfishness must be removed; otherwise, crime will continue to increase as selfish politicians and lawmakers commit public crimes against a people who are too blind to see it or too divided to do something about it. At the same time, the man at the bottom will continue to rise up and commit private crimes against a nation who ends up spending more of its tax dollars trying to flush him out. And let's not forget about that child somewhere who has to face the fact that he has to go into debt to enter college and then try to make it to the three percent of college graduates who actually find success! We can only hope that he doesn't become another enemy from within.

Chapter 6

Drugging the New Generation

Each generation that comes forward is wiser than the last generation. That's because of all the information afforded to us through the different media outlets. Generations and generations ago, a person only knew as much as their school and their parents taught them. Today's youth are learning from television, radio and via the Internet.

As each generation gets wiser, they are more and more deceived. Men learn to trust in their own artificial intelligence rather than trusting in the WORD of GOD. Not only does mass media produce entertainment for our youth, mass media is making followers of our youth. Please understand that almost every child looks up to someone, even the one who seems stand-offish and self-reliant. As children struggle to find their own identities, they look to mass media for different identities to try on. Pay attention to each era in music, for example. You will see that the costumes that our children wear as normal everyday gear has changed as new faces came on the music scene. People tend to channel people they idolize. Of course, to idolize someone is sin, because it simply means to make an idol of them.

As Hollywood employs more and more evil souls, the arena of entertainment is becoming darker. This is causing the youth to become evil, because a devilish celebrity is simply someone who makes sin look good. One thing about sin is it feels good when wearing it. It makes the person feel almost invincible and as if they have purpose. As the youth become more and more corrupt, scientists are bringing in more and more money as they "discover" new ways to identify personalities. Let the truth be told: they aren't identifying mental illnesses as they claim to do; they are identifying the behaviors of demonic spirits.

All the same, if you familiarize yourself with the world of legal drugs and the science behind them, you will find that many of the ailments that have been registered as actual diseases do not exist. They are simply personality traits that you find in certain individuals, while some diseases are the characteristics of the dark forces inhabiting that person.

There are certain behaviors that are characteristic to a cat that you would not find in a dog. There are certain characteristics found in one individual person that you won't find in another individual person. There are certain characteristics found in men that are not found in women, and vice versa. The powers of this world work the say way. Satan's followers (demonic forces, powers and principalities) operate by rank. There are the imp powers, which basically are just the lowest-ranking, but most common demonic forces). Imps operate everyday by possessing unbelievers or seducing believers. Of course, when we are saved, we become the temple of the HOLY SPIRIT and therefore, cannot be "possessed" by any other spirit. Nevertheless, when a demon can't get on the inside, it stands guard on the outside if it is permitted in through sin. It then becomes a stronghold against the mind of the believer. Everyday sins that we tend to commit open doors into our lives that permit these spirits to toy with us. Everyday sins include worry, doubt, perverse speech, fear and so on. They can't attack a person physically because they don't live in a physical body. Against the believer, demons and powers use the art of suggestion and lack of knowledge. So what they do is simply mess with the person's mind by making suggestions to them. They do this through media, personal relationships and through our imaginations. A believer has to believe something in order to receive it. To believe doesn't just mean to accept as true; to believe means to reject any other report other than the one you are believing in. To believe something means to receive it and let it reside in your heart as truth.

The Bible tells us that JESUS CHRIST is the Truth, and with the heart we believe. We receive CHRIST by believing in CHRIST and confessing HIM as our LORD and SAVIOR. That's why GOD warned us to guard our hearts, for out of it flow the issues of life. Satan tries to get us to believe in lies he has created and to confess those lies as truth, thus denying CHRIST JESUS. That way, he can reside in our hearts and flow from our lives to contaminate other believers and discourage unbelievers from accepting JESUS CHRIST into their hearts.

The wile you will see in operation now is the drugging of the next generation. Science and research have replaced the "in GOD we trust" motto that America once stood for, and our children don't know where to turn anymore. Nowadays, the media corrupts them, the food industry poisons them, and the government drugs them. This is America's attempt to become people-sufficient rather than depend on GOD at any cost. The issue is, has been, and will always be (until the return of our LORD, CHRIST JESUS), the love of money. As the Bible warns us, the love of money is the root of all evil. Money itself is not evil; it is the *love* of money that is evil. Simply put, this country makes more money nowadays by producing drugs and diagnosing "mental" problems than it has ever done! Those at the top of the totem pole have found new ways to make money!

Understand that most of what you see behavior-wise is coming from the parents (generational mindsets), media, peer pressure (bad association) or the chemicals and dyes used in foods today. For example, hyperactivity is linked to ADHD. Red dyes in foods are linked to hyperactivity. A parent who doesn't know that they are literally poisoning their child will often take them to a psychiatrist to be evaluated and to get a prescription to "cure" that child's behavior. The medicine is man-made or **man**ufactured; it's another chemical that's placed in the child's body. There are no medications that "cure" mental illnesses, because these problems aren't rooted in brain abnormalities; they are often simple issues that can be corrected by changing the diet, changing the channel and changing the mind.

Changing the Diet: A lot of what we eat is filled with poisons that the FDA says are healthy. Some foods even contain small amounts of arson! It is no wonder children (and adults) have behavioral issues.

Changing the Channel: Let's face it even if we don't want to. This generation is more wicked than the last generation because of what they are taking in media-wise. Each new generation of artists are more perverse and more profane than the last generation. Of course, they'd argue that they are not responsible for how you are raising your kids, and to some degree, they are right! You shouldn't let your kids listen to their music! You shouldn't let your kids watch their shows; you shouldn't let your kids make idols of mere imperfect men!

Changing the Mind: Your television set came with an operator's manual, your car came with an operator's manual, your electronic toothbrush likely came with an operator's manual, and you came with an operator's manual called the Holy Bible. If you put a car in reverse with the intent of going forward, you obviously don't know how to operate the car. You need to read your manual. Your children need the WORD of GOD to operate; otherwise, they will operate in reverse. Education is good, but you have to make sure that your children get that which is better: the WORD of GOD. And I'm not just talking about reading the Bible to them "sometimes" or just taking them to church on Sunday. They need to hear the WORD every day of their lives (just like you do), and they need to understand the purpose of the church building. Church was not created to simply teach people the WORD; church is for encouraging, sharpening and coming together with our Christian brethren. The learning part should mostly be done at home! *"Teach a youth about the way he should go; even when he is old he will not depart from it"* *(Proverbs 22:6)*.

When you teach the WORD to your children, you are giving them something FAR greater than a college education: you are giving them what they need to survive. Without the WORD, they will likely turn to something or someone to fill that GOD-sized hole in their hearts. We are designed by HIM for HIM; without HIM, we cannot find peace, joy or any of the blessings associated with HIM.

This worldly system is going to continue to diagnose disorders and diseases, just like they'll keep feeding poison to the mind and bodies of our children; nevertheless, it's up to you and me to feed them with the WORD and refuse to let anything unlike GOD enter their thinking systems or bodies. Remember this: This government and its setup are all about money; it is a capitalistic setup designed for the rich, supported by the middle-class and justified by the poor. Don't get yourself or your children caught up in depending on this worldly system; depend on the LORD.

Chapter 7

<u>Chained to Debt</u>

When I turned eighteen years old, I was bombarded by credit card offers. I was now legally a woman who could be held responsible for my adult actions; but at the same time, I was too immature to understand the burden of debt. So I saw a shopping spree as an opportunity to indulge my youthful lusts, and I could pay them back later in small increments. I was sold before the envelope was even opened.

At first, the bill didn't seem so bad. I would

shop like a mad woman and pay them the minimum to stay in good standing. I begin to notice that my bill almost remained the same, even though I was paying on it. I became frustrated with the fact that the interest fees seemed to swallow my minimum payments whole. After a while, my youthful thinking took over. What were they going to do to me if I should not pay? They were going to put it on my credit report; but at the time, that seemed to be no big deal. After all, I had plenty of time before I would consider home ownership. That's what I thought credit was for. My payments became smaller and smaller until they simply stopped. My bills were increasing as I aged, but my pay was barely inching up by the year. With no college education, I found myself heading down the path towards poverty fast.

Years later, I got married and found out the real

reason for credit. I worked and struggled trying to get the house of my dreams, only to be turned away again and again. Of course, his credit was no knight in shining armor either. Finally, after much prayer and applying what I was taught at church; we finally landed the house of our dreams. But those bills were swallowing us whole. We had the appearance of wealth, but not the reality of it. Our minds were set to look wealthy, all the while borrowing money to do so.

As I matured, I began to feel victimized by a system that requires that I have an education to get a decent job, but I don't have to be educated about debt. Suddenly, the reality set in: The set-up of the American (worldly) system gave off an appearance of nobility, but the reality was, it really requires that you get educated in helping those at the top become richer, but if you don't pay them back from the debt you owe to them, you would be punished greatly. Now, don't get me wrong; I totally agree that we should pay back our debt to one another; however, young adults should not be handed a credit card without first being educated about debt.

Then there is college. From the time we could understand our parents' voices, we have heard about this grand building that we'd go into someday and come out as a success. Our parents would show us doctors and lawyers and tell us about the big building that would help us to become these great men and women of society. We were prepped throughout elementary and high school for our journeys into the big building where all of the successful people in life had once ventured into. We watched our relatives head off to college, and we have admired them as they entered those double doors; those doors we knew they'd exit one day as a success story. Fast forward to adulthood. Most of the people who have been to college only came out with debt and plans to get another degree someday. Student loans are the monsters of debt that make getting the job in one's field pointless unless you graduated in a field where you'd earn enough to be nominated for upper middle-class. All the same, only 27 percent of college graduates actually find work in the fields they majored in.

So, what happens next? Another young adult is released into a society burdened down by debt and a job that refuses to pay them enough money to make a living. Why is that? Because your debt is someone else's residual income! What exactly is residual income? If you've ever had some charismatic multilevel marketing representative on the other end of your phone, you'd know this term well. It often refers to money that continues to come to you for the rest of your life based on a sale or service you performed at some point in time. According to TheBusinessDictionary.com, residual income is another name for recurring income, and it is defined as: *Compensation received for work after it has been completed on a reoccurring basis. This type of income stream allows for a person to continue receiving payments for the same work on a continual basis.*

Imagine if someone was indebted to you for the rest of their lives, or for a lengthy period of time. In hindsight, they'd be your slave until the debt was paid off. TheFreeDictionary.com defines slave as:

1. (Law) a person legally owned by another and having no freedom of action or right to property (Ref: TheFreeDictionary.com)

Need to Know: When you are indebted to

someone, you are legally owned by that person. How is that? Anything you earn may be taken from you to pay off that debt. It doesn't matter if you end up homeless and penniless; if you are in debt to someone, they have power over you. In some cases, you may even be imprisoned (IRS debt) if you do not pay. This means that you basically sell the rights to yourself physically and financially when you go into debt.

2. A person under the domination of another person or some habit or influence (Ref: TheFreeDictionary.com)

Need to Know: You will always be dominated by your debtor until you are released from your debt. Debtors often dominate those who are in debt to them by logging items on their credit reports, auditing their paychecks, and through harassment. All the same, even if you keep your payments up, other debtors may refuse to do business with you because of current debt.

3. (Business / Industrial Relations & HR Terms) a person who works in harsh conditions for low pay

(Ref: TheFreeDictionary.com)

Need to Know: This definition just described more than half of the American population.

But what does any of this have to do with you? It's simple; when you borrow from this worldly system, you become a slave of the system and those who run it. You literally become the property of the rich until you have learned to become GOD-dependent.

What is the American dream? By the time the average American gets into his or her mid to late 30s, they are up to their chin in debt. Nevertheless, they live in the house that they are buying, the car that they have bought, the children that they are raising, and the dog, who completes the family circle. If their debt is manageable, they have what is referred to as the American dream. Debt of any form is slavery, and debt is encouraged in this nation, because the people who enslave others are slaves to the love of money.

I went to a dealer's website one day and priced a new Nissan vehicle. I filled out the form and asked the dealer for the total price with taxes and whatever fees they'd add on so that I would know how much to save. I had been saving for a new vehicle because I had gotten accustomed to living a life where my husband and I were only indebted to pay rent, utilities and car insurance. I've learned to detest unnecessary monthly payments, especially after having once been a slave to debt.

When I awoke the next day, I saw an email from the dealership. One of the salesmen wanted to speak with me over the phone, and I agreed. Over the next few days, we kept playing phone tag with one another. He'd call while I was asleep, and I'd call when he had another customer. During these few days, I received countless emails from him. Finally, he called one day just as I was preparing to go to bed. (I often sleep during the day because I often work during the night). We exchanged the usual pleasantries, and then he asked me a few questions. I made it clear that I wanted to buy a particular vehicle with cash, and that I didn't want to finance or lease it. Honestly, I thought he'd be happy and want to do business with me, but my request seemed to somehow agitate him. I'll try to list the dialogue below. It's not verbatim, as I can't remember the entire dialogue, but I'll summarize it here:

Me: No, I want to get the full price of the vehicle because I am saving up to come and buy it with cash.

Salesmen: *(Sighs)* You mean with taxes, title

and all those other fees?

Me: Yes, sir.

Salesmen: *(Sighs)* Well, I will have to get with my manager to come up with a full fee, but let me ask you this: Why do you want to pay for it with cash? Have you considered financing?

Me: I don't like monthly payments.

Salesmen: *(Grunts)* Yeah, I understand that, but....*(sighs)*, we lose fifteen hundred dollars that way.

Me: *(Thinks to self: And?)* Okay.

Salesmen: I mean, you could finance it and pay it off as fast as you want. Not to mention, that particular vehicle will likely sell out soon, so it's better to come and get one while we still have them.

Me: I understand, but I intend to buy one with cash. My husband and I don't like debt.

Salesmen: *(Chews gum and sighs loudly).* Okay. I'll get with my manager and see if I can put something together and give you a full price. Keep in mind that we lose fifteen hundred dollars in cash-only deals. I have your email, so I'll contact you that way.

Me: Okay. Thanks.

I hung up the line puzzled. I thought a salesman would be ecstatic about having a customer come in and pay cash for a vehicle. Maybe it's because I'd never owned a brand new vehicle in my whole life. Before I met my husband, every vehicle I purchased was basically rent-to-own. After I met my husband, my vehicle renting days were over. He was and is totally against unnecessary debt, and at first I didn't understand why. "If we can't afford to pay for it with cash; we won't have it!" That was his loud declaration when I would oppose him with my "monthly" mentality. After all, we had to pay the rent once a month, the utilities once a month, and I had that monthly visitor who made me pay for the right to be called a

woman. What was a car note to me?
Hopefully, I could get the car note when I was
cramping; that way my attitude would be
justifiable.

Of course, the salesmen never emailed me
back. Why was that? Because even though
they would earn a profit from the sale of the
car, they wouldn't earn as much. When you go
into a dealership and finance a car; oftentimes
the dealership doesn't do in-house financing.
They go through a lot of creditors and banking
institutions to finance your vehicle. They
submit their price to the lender, and the lender
goes by the book value on the vehicle.
Oftentimes, the book value is greater than the
actual value of a vehicle based on the
condition of that vehicle; nevertheless, the
lender is not always aware. After all, once you
sign that agreement, you are locked in, and the
car is off the seller's hands. You now have an

agreement between you and the lender. At the same time, whenever a dealer has in-house financing, he stands to earn the price of the vehicle plus the interest, but he runs a greater risk. What if you don't pay for the vehicle? Companies who do in-house financing often don't have enough money to sue you; therefore, they harass you. If you pay it out, he wins; if you don't pay it out, he loses big. So, the dealer did not want to deal with me because they'd already priced their vehicles plus the financing. They weren't willing to sell the vehicle without me going into some form of bondage to them.

Is buying a car month-to-month a bad idea? No, it isn't. But if you can afford to pay it out, why not just knock out the payment and move on to the next blessing on GOD'S list? Why be in bondage to someone else, driving "their" vehicle and paying them monthly? Why pay the hiked up insurance rates that are associated with rent-to-own or leased vehicles? Some people would reason that financing frees up a lot of their money, but many don't consider how much money they end up tying up in this deal. It's not just the vehicle you have to consider; you also have to consider the change in lifestyle that is made to afford those monthly payments. You have to consider the sacrifices, the extra hours at work, and every other stress or inconvenience associated with monthly payments.

The Bible tells us that a good man leaves an inheritance to his children and his children's children. *(See Proverbs 13:22).* What you and I should be doing as adults is building a future for our children and teaching them to build a future for their children. That way, they wouldn't have to depend on someone else to loan them the money for their education; they wouldn't get caught up in this web that most of them will never get out of. When they have to depend on the world's system, they too get caught up in it and begin to depend on it. They then toss their children into this web to grow up as vagabonds and slaves. Oftentimes, many don't realize their positions because they are so distracted by the things of this world that they don't see the chains about them. They window shop for the next set of shackles to wear for the next three to seven years or more.

The Bible warns us about the world's system. We are rapidly approaching a time where the system of this world will be so dark that it will openly profess its disdain for GOD. Everything associated with CHRIST is slowly being wiped out, and slaves are being made each and every day as the American dream continues to be redefined without the "in GOD we trust" motto. We are coming up in a lust-filled generation where we are able to indulge in the things of this world, but at the price of servitude. We can now have that new model Lexus that we so desire, but first, we must sign on the dotted line. Understand this: It's okay to need a vehicle; it's normal to need clothing, and who doesn't need food? But wisdom will teach you to build for the Kingdom of GOD according to the talents in which HE has given you and THEN shop wisely. As you get more wisdom, knowledge and understanding, you will find that those lustful desires to have the things you can't afford will diminish because you will transition from being a follower to a leader. You will follow after CHRIST, but you will lead a generation into a new mindset where they can indulge in the fruits of the SPIRIT, as opposed to the **man**ufactured produce of man. One day, you'll find yourself able to afford that new Lexus, but you may not want it anymore, because wisdom has now taken the spot where coveting once sat. A rich man who has earned his wealth doesn't always like fancy things; as a matter of fact, wealthy people don't indulge as much as people in poverty. Wealthy people invest; a poor man spends. Wealthy people invest in providing the products and services that a poor man spends to have.

You will find that life is so much easier without the unnecessary monthly baggage that many are now buried under. After you escape that mentality for a year or so, you will never desire to go back under it because there is something about being free that's addictive. There is something about being free that makes you notice the colors on the trees; that makes you walk a little slower to enjoy the rumble of the grass and that makes you smile as the wind kisses your face each day. At the same time, there is something about being bound that makes you want to curse everyone out, toss down a ton of sugar a day and throw rocks at free men while you wish for the day when you will be granted your freedom.

It's not difficult; do the research yourself and see just how long you have been chained to debt, and then set your date of release. Abide by it and never return to debt. If you can afford to buy something with cash, do so. Use the extra money to invest in your businesses or whatever GOD has you invest into. Do without the luxuries when you cannot afford them. Don't get caught up in the mindset of trying to wear the appearance of wealth, because people who do this often end up being worn out by lack. Instead, take the time out to be as unique and peculiar as GOD created you to be, and save towards your future. If you can't afford something, do without it for now if you don't need it. Most of what we finance is things we could have done without.

When my husband and I first moved to Florida, we didn't have any money or furniture to furnish our new apartment, so we had to sit on the floor. We had a blow-up mattress to sleep on, and that was it. I was immature at that time, and still saw borrowing as a blessing. I told my husband I wanted us to go to a furniture store and buy (month-to-month) a couch and a bed, but he refused. He kept saying that if we could not afford to pay cash for it, we wouldn't have it. I threw a temper-tantrum because I did not understand. To me, it was simple. We were waking up with backaches from that air mattress, and we had to sit on the carpet every day, propping ourselves up against the wall. All we had to do was go down to a furniture store, pay a little money down and let them fix our problems by bringing us some furniture. He wouldn't hear of it, and I wouldn't stop talking about it.

Finally, one day he came home and said we had enough to go and buy a bed, but not a mattress. A co-worker of his had taken us down to a local IKEA a couple of weekends before that, and we'd picked out a bed that we intended to come back and purchase. The bed was $299 when we'd went the first time, but when we went back to purchase it, it was on sale for $199! We were excited, and I just praised the LORD because we were able to afford to buy a mattress as well, since our bed didn't need a box spring. A few months later, we had enough cash to buy a couch, and we did. Nowadays, I am thankful that we didn't do monthly payments because they would have been a huge burden on us while we were in that time of transitioning. Since then, I have learned to live without creating debt, and I love the freedom of not having that mental burden of keeping up with who I owe. This is indeed the freedom that CHRIST wants for all of HIS people.

Chapter 8

The Wealth of the Wicked Is Laid Up

"A good man leaveth an inheritance to his children's children: and the wealth of the sinner is laid up for the just" (Proverbs 13:22).

Sometimes, we read scriptures religiously and miss the substance therein. There is so much to Proverbs 13:22 that has been overlooked by many who have read it. First off, the Bible tells us that a "good" man leaves an inheritance to his children's children. Who is a "good" man? Could that wealthy Atheist be a good man

113

because he died and left millions of dollars and countless properties to his children? No. Leaving money to a child avails him nothing if you don't leave behind the wisdom of how to earn more money and how to keep that money. More than that, children need the wisdom to survive and the knowledge of CHRIST. Leaving a million dollars to a child with no attachment of wisdom is like leaving a loaded gun in a toy box. So what is it that makes a man "good" when he leaves an inheritance for his grandchildren? It's simple. The Bible was written for the believer. When a child of GOD is blessed with material riches, it only means that he was blessed with the substance (wisdom) to not only obtain those riches, but he was blessed with wisdom...period! Wisdom is like an armored car that transports around your riches and keeps you safe. Wisdom is the wealthy suit that GOD gives us to wear before HE blesses us with material wealth. After all, material things are not the actual blessings; they are the evidence that we are blessed! Understand this: A wise man doesn't have to possess millions of dollars and fancy homes to be rich. He has direct access to the account of GOD, and he can tap in through faith whensoever he pleases! He can never go broke because FATHER has given him something far greater than access to a credit card with no spending limit; HE gave him the ability to obtain wealth, create wealth, and call wealth by name whenever he so pleases! At the same time, he can call peace, joy, health, longevity, mercy and any other blessings that GOD offers HIS elect. Not having wealth in his sight is not the same as not having access to wealth. Everything in the earth is under a righteous man's dominion, and he can call whatever he wants to call as long as it is in the will of GOD. In the will of GOD means that it is a part of our inheritance; therefore, we cannot call wickedness upon ourselves or others; we can only call the blessings of GOD upon ourselves and others.

I dealt with a few situations where money was stolen from me. In these situations, I had hired or entrusted someone to do work for me and the work was not done, my money was not returned (by them), and I just shrugged it off. I remember talking to a family member about it, and she was beside herself telling me to take these individuals to court. I smiled and told her that GOD had already shown me how to get back what belongs to me. I had a mouth; I had the faith, so all I had to do was call it back. I began to speak to the money and commanded it to come back to me in JESUS Name. Each time, I got the money back from another direction and GOD also gave me interest on that money! It didn't come back from the people who'd taken it; it came back through other avenues. How did I know it was my money from those situations? GOD has a special way of giving you your money back and letting you know where it is coming from. Therefore, I was able to release them from their debt in my heart so that they could be indebted to CHRIST! That's how forgiveness works! It works the same way as going into a loan company and borrowing money from them. If you refuse to pay the money back, they will oftentimes sell your account to a debt collector who will add interest to the account and come after you legally. By the time they've finished with you, you will have paid more than double of what you originally owed. The loan company will forgive you because the debt is no longer on their desks to be collected; it is in the hands of the collection agency. CHRIST is our collection agency! Anything that is owed to you has ears to hear you. Anything that GOD has given to you has your name on it, and you have the right to call it back to you as long as it is done in JESUS Name, and you release the debt to HIM! HE will pay you back, and then HE will go after them. That's the way it works!

A good man not only leaves wisdom to his children; he leaves them with instruction. He also leaves them in the hands of GOD, and he trusts the LORD to lead them in his absence. It is better for a man who is poor materially to leave wisdom, knowledge and understanding to his son than it is for a rich man to leave wealth to his son with no wisdom, knowledge or understanding to back it. *"For what shall it profit a man, if he shall gain the whole world, and lose his own soul?" (Mark 8:36).*

What exactly is the "wealth of the sinner?" GOD is the Almighty CREATOR; HE has created all things in Heaven and in earth. We are HIS creations, created in HIS image;

therefore, we are creative. Even the sinner is creative because he was created by the CREATOR. Many sinners are gifted, but because they are perverted, they have perverted the use of their gifts. All the same, they still have gifts, and many of them acquire the knowledge of how to get wealth. They are still called of GOD; they just haven't answered the call on their lives. *"For the gifts and calling of God are without repentance" (Romans 11:29).* Therefore, the wealth of the sinner is the call they have upon their lives and the knowledge they have to obtain the blessings of GOD. Because they have chosen another path, what GOD has laid up for them will become the double, triple, quadruple or seven-fold portion of the believer who has chosen to follow CHRIST. Again, all you have to do is call the blessings, and they will answer you if you have answered the call upon your life.

There was another time where I had been pushing so many people to tap into the gifts that GOD had given them. I interviewed people, nudged people and testified of the goodness of the LORD. What I found was that the average believer has a stronghold called procrastination blocking their pathways to wealth. At the end of these pathways is what I think of as a refrigerator with a lock on it, but the key to open it is obedience. In pushing people, I found myself being pushed back by the excuses they had. Some of them were up front that they were fighting procrastination; others used the "it's not my season" argument, as if gifts are seasonal. Suddenly, the realization came in that these people are throwing away something far more precious than silver and gold! They were throwing away their ability to obtain and keep wealth, so I asked the LORD to give me every gift they had <u>that they were not going to use</u>. Why let it go to waste? After that, I found myself tapping into new gifts, new knowledge and new blessings. Did I steal their gifts? No. I simply let the LORD know that I would obey HIM with their gifts, and **IF** they were going to go to waste, to just give them to me. Why is this point important? As a believer, you need to know how to get wealth, and you need to know that there is wealth laying around you. If you could see in the spirit, you would find yourself trying to step over (and not being able to) all of the gifts and callings that the saints are throwing away just to go under a system that they trust more than they trust GOD. I'm not kidding you when I say there is wealth to be had all over the place! All GOD needs is a faithful saint who will utilize his own gifts faithfully and bless the LORD with them, and HE will continue to add onto this servant. *"He that is faithful in that which is least is faithful also in much: and he that is unjust in the least* *is unjust also in much" (Luke 16:10).*

Another sword many believers fall under is emulation. Merriam-Webster defines emulation this way:

- obsolete: ambitious or envious rivalry
- ambition or endeavor to equal or excel others (as in achievement)
- imitation

Many believers are emulating the success of others because they trust more in the works than they do in the LORD. In more than half of the mentoring sessions I have done with believers, I have found that the large majority of them were emulating someone else. They saw one man start an Internet phone company, and they tried to start an Internet phone company. They saw one woman find her wealthy place in styling hair, and suddenly they wanted to start their own salons. This happens even in ministry! I have a graphics company where I create and sell Bishop seals, logos and websites, and I often come in contact with people who will not shop my store for what's available (seals and logos); they go directly to my portfolio because they are only moved to buy something when they see that someone else has it. Once I told them that the ones in my portfolio already belonged to someone and we guaranteed them an exclusive design, I have literally lost potential customers! Before that, I would ask them if they had checked out the store on the site; after all, there are more than 700 available designs (currently) in the store, and in more than 97% of the cases, they said no! They wanted to shop the portfolio because they are moved to buy things that belong to others; they don't like anything original because they trust the lead of others, and they like to emulate others. At the same time, there were countless times when I had customers who wanted a website created. They would show me the websites of other ministries and boldly tell me that they wanted their websites designed exactly the same way that another man or woman's site was designed. When I told them that my company did not duplicate the designs of others, and that we could design them something far greater than the sites they were coveting, they didn't want to hear it. They went to other companies who would happily feed their envy. People of GOD, you will never find your wealth in another man's yard. Whatever GOD gives to you is HIS, but HE names you as the person (inheritor) to carry out that assignment. In doing so, the wealth and acknowledgment (inheritance) is often given to you; therefore, you are blessed in obedience! Any time you find yourself trying on the anointing of another person, you are asking to try on the trials and tribulations that person had to endure to perfect their gifts. What happens when you call unused, tossed out and neglected gifts to you? Will you try on their trials and tribulations? Not always. Sometimes their trials and tribulations came upon them as a result of their choices. All the same, they probably wouldn't have had to go through those trials and tribulations had they tapped into the gifts and callings on their lives, but when the gifts are on your doorstep, you will probably endure the tests if you don't know how to open them properly. Anytime you emulate someone else, you are operating as the "wicked".

- **James 3:16**- *"For where envying and strife is, there is confusion and every evil work."*

- **1 Corinthians 3:3**- *"For ye are yet carnal: for whereas there is among you envying, and strife, and divisions, are ye not carnal, and walk as men?"*

By the way, the Bible uses "envying" and "emulations" interchangeably. Some translations refer to it as envying, while other translations refer to it as emulations.

If you are emulating someone else, you are neglecting the gifts and calling on your life! You are electing to disregard who you are to run a touchdown for another team. Nobody's gift will open doors for you unless the LORD hands that gift to you because they have rejected it! *"A man's gift makes room for him, and brings him before great men" (Proverbs 18:16).* Rejecting a gift is like rejecting your own baby! You carry it throughout the gestation period, labor with it; but somehow, you don't bond with it; and when it is born, you abandon it as if it were of no value. Understand that GOD gave each gift a name, and these gifts are precious to HIM; therefore, HE will not let them stay buried. Instead, HE will hand them to someone who is faithful, and HE will let them reap the blessings from them. *"After a long time the lord of those servants cometh, and reckoneth with them. And so he that had received five talents came and brought other five talents, saying, Lord, thou deliveredst unto me five talents: behold, I have gained beside them five talents more. His lord said unto him, Well done, thou <u>good and faithful</u> servant: <u>thou hast been faithful over a few things</u>, **I will make thee ruler over many things**: enter thou into the **joy of thy lord**"* (Matthew 25:19-21). All the same, the above scripture gives us an understanding as to why some people do not have the joy of the LORD. The joy of the LORD is found in obedience! I remember having a friend who would go into a state of depression anytime she wasn't tapping into the calling on her life. Whenever she would start being obedient again, she would shine and her voice would quiver with joy. If you want to obtain wealth, tap into your gifts and answer the call on your life!

Money has ears to hear. How do we know this? 2 Chronicles 1:12 reads, "*Wisdom and knowledge is granted unto thee; and I will give thee riches, and wealth, and honour, such as none of the kings have had that have been before thee, neither shall there any after thee have the like.*" How does GOD work? HE calls those things which be not as though they were. Anything GOD has created has ears to hear HIM, and HE has commanded the wealth of the wicked to be laid up for the just. GOD calls the wealth; it answers the call and waits for you in obedience.

But what if the wealth is in the hands of the wicked? Will it answer GOD, or is there new wealth being created to come and bless you? Wealth is already a Kingdom promise to the elect of GOD; therefore, it is already within the realm of the earth. Oftentimes, wealth will find itself in the hands of the wicked, but because it has ears to hear the LORD, it will answer HIS call. That's why so many people who are unfaithful can never seem to catch a break. Income tax season comes around, and they get a hefty check of $10,000. While the check is in the mail, their cars suddenly break down or the roof in their homes suddenly gives and has to be repaired. Now that check that is on its way is only stopping through to visit them on its way to you, the faithful. They pay the mechanic to fix their cars; they pay the roofing specialist to fix their rooftops, and the money goes into the hands of these individuals. If they are faithful servants of GOD, money will adhere to GOD and start to act as a seed in their lives. If they are unfaithful, something else will happen to where that money will find its way out of their grasps and back on the

129

road looking for its way back to you, the faithful. Once it has found its way back to the faithful, it rests and acts as a seed. They can then obey GOD and sow seeds into the lives of others, their ministries or wherever GOD commands them to sow a seed. When they sow that seed, they are simply impregnating fertile ground. In doing so, more wealth is born to them, and the wealth continues to grow as long as they are faithful.

Finally, we understand that the wealth of the sinner is laid up or reserved for the "just." What does it mean to be just? Just is short for justice. It means to be fair-minded and unbiased. To give wealth to an unjust man is to give wealth to the wicked, because an unjust man will not be fair. An unjust man will try to increase his wealth by giving to the wealthy and ignoring the poor. *"He that oppresseth the poor to increase his riches, and he that giveth*

to the rich, shall surely come to want"
(Proverbs 22:16). In giving to the rich, he is
trusting in his own devices and has tapped into
the very nature of Satan: selfishness. Because
of this, he becomes unjust, and his wealth
starts utilizing creative ways to get away from
him. *"Wilt thou set thine eyes upon that which*
is not? For riches certainly make themselves
wings; they fly away as an eagle toward
heaven" (Proverbs 23:5).

Again, wealth is not always money. Wealth
can divorce a man and still leave him rich in
material possessions. Find him without the
wealth (fruits of the Spirit), and you will find a
mad man with health problems and a million
dollars that has no power or desire to bail him
out. And then he still has hell to look forward
to.

Do you want to tap into your wealthy place?

Remember these pointers.

- **The wealth of the wicked is laid up for the just.** The wealth of the believer is not laid up for you, so don't try to tap into your brother's or sister's anointings. Instead, ask the LORD to give you the wealth of the wicked so that you may glorify HIS Name with it. All the same, ask HIM to give you the gifts that other believers around you have and **<u>will not</u>** use. Again, if they are going to eventually tap into them, HE won't give those gifts to you and you shouldn't want them.

- **Make sure your motive is right in wanting those gifts.** If you want them to glorify GOD, your heart is in the right place. If you want them to glorify yourself, your heart has a dark spot that has to be removed.

- **Do not emulate others.** Who you are

will usher you into your wealthy place.
When you try to emulate someone else,
you will often find yourself falling under
the trials and tests that were reserved
for that person. Remember, they were
created to go through and overcome;
you were not.

- **Be faithful with the gifts you have
  before you ask for more.** There is
  nothing more overwhelming than having
  a plate full of to-dos and no drive to do
  them.

- **Keep your heart pure.** Occasionally,
  you just have to be strange with yourself
  and ask yourself some pretty pointed
  questions. Sometimes, I find that pride
  will rise up in me and try to hide the
  Truth (CHRIST) behind a justification.
  To get the Truth (CHRIST) to come
  forward, I ask myself a question, and I
  answer back with the Truth. I always

know when pride (darkness) is there because I will often stumble over the Truth, trying to pacify whatever lusts have risen up in me. Finally, I will let the Truth come forward, and I renounce whatever darkness came in and tried to cover up my Light (CHRIST). It may sound silly, but it works.

- **Do NOT put your trust in this world.** The world has absolutely nothing to offer a believer. After all, you are due an inheritance from GOD. What can top that?

- **Get busy doing whatever GOD told you to do.** Most believers will say that they will get busy in their gifts and callings, but these are words that they have spoken before. If you are going to get busy, start right now!

- **Invest in whatever GOD gave you.** Understand that the word "investment" is just a professional word for "seed." Sow seeds into the gifts and call on your life, and GOD will increase you.

- **Don't be impatient; every seed has its season.** You can't plant a tree today and expect to climb it tomorrow. Some seeds take longer to grow than others. The ones that take longer often grow up to be taller and live longer than the ones that shot up almost immediately. Let the seasons play out, and you just continue to trust GOD and sow more seeds. *"A faithful man shall abound with blessings: but he that maketh haste to be rich shall not be innocent" (Proverbs 28:20).*

- **Loan GOD some money; give to the poor.** Wait a minute. Does GOD really need a loan? No. HE needs faithful people with a heart of love in the earth realm who are willing to bless HIS people. *"He that hath pity upon the poor* *lendeth unto the LORD; and that which he hath given will he pay him again"* *(Proverbs 19:17).*

- **Be a cheerful giver, and give because you love and trust HIM; not because you need something.** Some people give with intent, and this is not good giving. We are to trust GOD in all things, but give in love. When you sow in tears, you reap in joy. What does that mean? Everything in the earth realm is a seed, and whatever grows up for us bears witness to the type of seed it is and the heart we sowed it with. When a man gives with a heart of love, even when he is grieved, he has taken off the selfish man and put on the heart of GOD. Because of this, he will reap in joy. If he sows a seed that he does not want to sow, it is because he trusts more in the seed than he trusts in the

One who gives life to that seed. At the same time, he wants something in return; therefore, he is trying to con GOD into giving him what he wants in return for him doing what GOD told him to do. *"Every man according as he purposeth in his heart, so let him give; not grudgingly, or of necessity: for God loveth a cheerful giver"* (2 Corinthians 9:7).

- **Be innovative!** Let's face it; any anointing GOD gives a man is unlike the anointing HE has given another man. Don't be afraid to be an agent of change; after all, GOD is peculiar, and so are you!

- **Be faithful...period!** Remember the parable of the talents. The faithful servants not only increased what they had, but they were excited to show the LORD what they'd earned. As a result,

HE blessed them.

- **Give...period!** *"Give, and it shall be given unto you; good measure, pressed down, and shaken together, and running over, shall men give into your bosom. For with the same measure that ye mete withal it shall be measured to you again"* *(Luke 6:38).*

- **Keep the faith!** Faith is so beautiful to GOD that HE accounted it to Abraham as righteousness! This means that even though Abraham didn't do all of the works of righteousness, he was given the cloak of righteousness, all because he believed GOD! *"And all things, whatsoever ye shall ask in prayer, believing, ye shall receive" (Matthew 21:22).*

- **Do NOT doubt GOD; doubt your situation!** It is normal to have doubt, but you have to know where to point that doubt. Doubt is like a loaded weapon. When you point it at GOD, you are saying you do not believe GOD, and this makes you like the unbeliever! Because of this, you will eat from the table of the unbeliever. When you point doubt at the enemy and his lies, you are essentially robbing him of the password you need to access your blessings. Understand that when GOD released them to you, they were already yours; you simply need to reach out in faith to grab them and pull them down with your praise. *"For verily I say unto you, That whosoever shall say unto this mountain, Be thou removed, and be thou cast into the sea; and shall not doubt in his heart, but shall believe that those things which he saith shall come to pass; he shall have whatsoever he saith"* (Mark 11:23).

- **Confess what you believe!** When your

parents told you they would buy you those new shoes you wanted, you confessed it to the world because you believed them! GOD is far better than your earthly parents, and HE wants to see an even greater faith on you towards HIM than you had towards your parents. *"For with the heart man believeth unto righteousness; and with the mouth confession is made unto salvation" (Romans 10:10).*

- **Know when to walk away from friends and family!** Let's face it; some people are just poisonous to our destinies. At the same time, some people will continue to speak death over what you are attempting to speak life into. Because of this, you may endure unnecessary warfare. Additionally, if you are a believer, you put people at risk by having a relationship with them that

GOD did not call you to have. How so? Gossipers gossip; therefore, they will draw their swords against you and reap the wrath of GOD. Slanderers slander; therefore, they will draw their swords against you and reap the already declared WORD of GOD. Some people can't have intimate access to anointed people, just the same as a rich man has to guard his wealth by not letting everyone have access to him. Sometimes, GOD will not allow you to access your wealthy place until you have let go of poisonous relationships. HE doesn't do this to punish you; HE does this to protect you! All the same, the wicked often put leashes on the people they associate with, and these people can never reach their blessings until they get off all fours and learn to walk upright! *"Be not deceived: evil*

communications corrupt good manners"
(1 Corinthians 15:33).

- **Ask for Wisdom; she always brings her friends Wealth and Honor with her!** Wisdom is spiritual wealth, and with it, you can never be poor...unless you choose to be. A poor wise man is not poor because he can't access material wealth; he is materially poor because he's too busy enjoying his spiritual wealth! *"And God said to Solomon, Because this was in thine heart, and thou hast not asked riches, wealth, or honour, nor the life of thine enemies, neither yet hast asked long life; but hast asked wisdom and knowledge for thyself, that thou mayest judge my people, over whom I have made thee king: Wisdom and knowledge is granted unto thee; and I will give thee riches, and wealth, and* *honour, such as none of the kings have had that have been before thee, neither shall there any after thee have the like"* *(2 Chronicles 1:11-12).*

Chapter 9

Capitalism vs. Lazarus

Capitalism:

a. An economic system in which the means of production and distribution are **privately or corporately owned** and development is proportionate to the accumulation and reinvestment of profits gained in a free market.

b. (Economics) an economic system based on the **private ownership** of the means of production, distribution, and exchange, characterized by the freedom of capitalists to operate or manage their property for profit in competitive conditions. *Also called free* *enterprise, private enterprise.*

Free Enterprise:

The freedom of private businesses to operate competitively for profit with minimal government regulation.

Private Enterprise:

1. Business activities unregulated by state ownership or control; privately owned business.

2. A privately owned business enterprise, especially one operating under a system of free enterprise or laissez-faire capitalism.

(Reference: The above definitions were taken from TheFreeDictionary.com).

Merriam Webster's definition of capitalism is: a way of **organizing an economy** so that the things that are used to make and transport products (such as land, oil, factories, ships, etc.) are **owned by individual people** and companies **rather than by the government**

As you can see, with a capitalistic government, the people are run and owned by those who own the wealth of this country. The majority of our government's decisions are based on "the people" as reported. But exactly what people are they based on? The ones who fund them, of course. It's not a white thing, a black thing or a brown thing; it's a money thing. Who helped your state representative to get into office by financing their campaign? Find them, and you'll find the puppet-masters.

The corruption of a people always starts with the love of money. Wherever the most money is, you will find the most influential power, but this is no godly power that's pulling the strings of a lot of this world's elected officials. *"For we wrestle not against flesh and blood, but against principalities, against powers, against the rulers of the darkness of this world, against* **_spiritual wickedness in high places_**" *(Ephesians 6:12).* The power you see in operation is demonic in nature. It's simple: In the world's system, money is power; therefore, godless souls apply GOD-given tactics to earn money. They have learned the art of sowing and reaping; nevertheless, this principal is discouraged amongst those who are not wealthy. How is this done? Wages paid to middle-class and lower-class individuals are oftentimes so low that the people cannot afford to sow; they simply finance. The wealthy, on the other hand, sow and finance. *"For the gifts and calling of God are without repentance" (Romans 11:29).* A wealthy man's idea of sowing is basically investing; nevertheless, there is a line that many of today's wealthiest people dance on. That line is sowing and gambling. There are many investments that can be written off as a seed sown such as buying property. It can still be looked at as a gamble, but it really is not a gamble because the person paid for land and got land in return. All the same, they may be hoping for or expecting the value of the land to increase, and that part is where the gambling begins, because there is no guarantee that it will increase. In gambling, you run the risk of not getting anything in return or losing what you have invested. Just like sowing a seed in church; you will receive a return if:

- Your seed was planted in obedience.
- Your seed was planted in good ground.
- Your seed was planted with joy.
- Your seed was planted with expectation.

Other than that, you abort the seed when you sow it the wrong way.

It's funny that the office of the senate is called

the U.S. Capitol. This is where the elected officials come together to vote on laws, pass bills, approve treaties, declare war and so on. But this is in no way a government for the people by the people; it is a government for the rich people by the poor people. The poor and middle-class are the hearts, ribs, backbones and legs of this country. We enter into wars that we don't want to enter into, but the senate makes this decision. So many of our wars are senseless, but there is a stand to gain financially in the long-haul; therefore, the men and women who signed up to protect this country are sent off into foreign lands to die for a rich man's desire to become richer. Most of the people who have died unnecessary deaths were under the guise that they were protecting their land, when in truth, they were not. They were told they were protecting the lives of others, when in truth, they were sent against nations to get revenge against a government who would not submit to this world's system or a government who had their own demonic system setup. It was and is all about money, and many people know this; nevertheless, most Americans remain quiet. After all, no one wants to be that "prisoner" who speaks out against a system that enslaves them, especially those who have learned to find comfort in their cells.

As the church, you must understand that the world's system was not created for or by you; it was created by man for the love of money. *"For the love of money is the root of all evil: which while some coveted after, they have erred from the faith, and pierced themselves through with many sorrows" (1 Timothy 6:10).* As the scriptures warn us, such individuals have:

- rooted themselves in evil
- erred or gone away from the faith

- pierced themselves with many sorrows

Why would you want to join hands with this world's system? Where do you see a place to set your feet in a system designed to watch people suffer and die so that those at the top can live better than kings and have more than enough to feed a country of men? They make their beds on the bodies of fallen soldiers; they set their tables on the backs of laborers who desire to at least eat the crumbs that fall from their tables; they bleed countries of their wealth and watch them starve to death because of their unquenchable greed. They have the bellies of hell; they are never satisfied with their wealth; they want more wealth, more power and more notoriety, and they are willing to kill to get it. They deceive nations and then slaughter them for their wealth. This is the reason GOD warned you not to join hands with this system; this is the reason GOD warned you that anyone who is a friend of the world is an enemy of HIS.

Luke 16:19-31 (NIV) reads:

"There was a rich man who was dressed in purple and fine linen and lived in luxury every day. At his gate was laid a beggar named Lazarus, covered with sores and longing to eat what fell from the rich man's table. Even the dogs came and licked his sores. The time came when the beggar died and the angels carried him to Abraham's side. The rich man also died and was buried. In Hades, where he was in torment, he looked up and saw Abraham far away, with Lazarus by his side. So he called to him, 'Father Abraham, have pity on me and send Lazarus to dip the tip of his finger in water and cool my tongue, because I am in agony in this fire.' But Abraham replied, 'Son, remember that in your lifetime you received your good things, while Lazarus received bad things, but now he is

comforted here and you are in agony. And besides all this, between us and you a great chasm has been set in place, so that those who want to go from here to you cannot, nor can anyone cross over from there to us.' He answered, 'Then I beg you, father, send Lazarus to my family, for I have five brothers. Let him warn them, so that they will not also come to this place of torment.' Abraham replied, 'They have Moses and the Prophets; let them listen to them.' 'No, father Abraham,' he said, 'but if someone from the dead goes to them, they will repent.' He said to him, 'If they do not listen to Moses and the Prophets, they will not be convinced even if someone rises from the dead.'"

Saints, this is the very same system and mindset that governs this world today. Sure, those who have a cold heart towards their brethren will be punished greatly, but this shouldn't be our wish. Our wish is that they come to repentance before it is too late. All the same, when the church bows down to this system and its mindset, the church has just chosen who it has allowed to follow. Whomever or whatever you submit to is lord of your life. You simply cannot serve two gods, and there are no words to camouflage what you are doing.

It's not that the world's system is against the poor; the error is that it is for the wealthy. *"One who oppresses the poor to increase his wealth and one who gives gifts to the rich--both come to poverty" (Proverbs 22:16 NIV).* What do you see happening to this system? America is in drowning in debt because the people with the remotes to it are self-centered and power-driven. They give to the rich and rob the poor of his gain. They create laws designed to keep "the people" out of their way while they continue to break these very laws.

We were supposed to be a nation under GOD, but because of greed, this nation has submitted itself to the dark powers of this world. Vanity is her name, and she is a whore of this world. She adorns herself with costly apparel and pretends to be a moral woman; but don't let her fool you. She is the mistress of Satan, abominable to GOD and full of darkness. Her breath is scented with the rot of the people she has consumed. Under her skirt, you will find the evidence of her whoredoms. She is the great whore that rides upon the beast in the book of Revelation. Revelation 17:1-18 reads:

*•And there came one of the seven angels which had the seven vials, and talked with me, saying unto me, Come hither; I will shew unto thee the judgment of the **great whore that sitteth upon many waters**:*

*•**With whom the kings of the earth have committed fornication**, and the **inhabitants***

of the earth have been made drunk with the wine of her fornication.

*•So he carried me away in the spirit into the wilderness: and I saw a woman sit upon a scarlet colored beast, **full of names of blasphemy**, having seven heads and ten horns.*

*•**And the woman was arrayed in purple and scarlet color, and decked with gold and precious stones and pearls, having a golden cup in her hand full of abominations and filthiness of her fornication:***

•And upon her forehead was a name written, MYSTERY, BABYLON THE GREAT, THE MOTHER OF HARLOTS AND ABOMINATIONS OF THE EARTH.

*•And I saw the woman **drunken with the blood of the saints**, and with the **blood of the martyrs of Jesus**: and when I saw her, **I wondered with great admiration.***

*•And the angel said unto me, **Wherefore didst***

thou marvel? *I will tell thee the mystery of the woman, and of the beast that carrieth her, which hath the seven heads and ten horns.*

•*The beast that thou sawest was, and is not; and shall ascend out of the bottomless pit, and go into perdition: and they that dwell on the earth shall wonder, whose names were not written in the book of life from the foundation of the world, when they behold the beast that was, and is not, and yet is.*

•*And here is the mind which hath wisdom. The seven heads are seven mountains, on which the woman sitteth.*

•***And there are seven kings: five are fallen, and one is, and the other is not yet come; and when he cometh, he must continue a short space.***

•*And the beast that was, and is not, even he is the eighth, and is of the seven, and goeth into perdition.*

•*And the ten horns which thou sawest are ten kings, which have received no kingdom as yet; but receive power as kings one hour with the beast.*

•***These have one mind, and shall give their power and strength unto the beast.***

•*These **shall make war with the Lamb**, and the **Lamb shall overcome them**: for he is Lord of lords, and King of kings: and **they that are with him are called, and chosen, and faithful.***

•*And he saith unto me, **The waters which thou sawest, where the whore sitteth, are peoples, and multitudes, and nations, and tongues.***

•*And the ten horns which thou sawest upon the beast, these shall hate the whore, and shall make her desolate and naked, and shall eat her flesh, and burn her with fire.*

•*For God hath put in their hearts to fulfill his*

will, and to agree, and give their kingdom unto the beast, until the words of God shall be fulfilled.

•*And* **the woman which thou sawest is that great city, which reigneth over the kings of the earth***.*

Who is the great whore who sits upon many waters? The world's system, of course. It is the very system that America leads and the world buys into. It is a system designed to slaughter those who oppose it and humiliate those who want out of it. It is a system that gives the green light to sin as long as it doesn't encroach upon wealthy territory. It is a system designed to capitalize on anything and anyone who can turn a profit in any way. It is a system that allows drugs into the United States and abroad because there are some people at the top of the totem pole who are benefiting from the crack and heroin addicts. Sure, the man

160

on the corner is arrested if he is caught selling drugs, but make no mistake about it: he's just a pawn in a larger game. This is a system who sells alcohol to the people knowing full well the effects of alcoholism. There is someone at the top of the totem pole who is benefiting from that drunk who took the life of that family man. According to the world's system, he is just another tragedy; nothing more than a casualty of war. Not a war against drugs and drunk driving; a tug-o-war between what's good and evil. Just throw a ribbon up somewhere along the highway and arrest the man who got "caught" driving drunk. His crime isn't being intoxicated behind the wheel; his crime is being caught. A crime is never a crime until you get caught committing it, but what is the purpose of selling alcohol? Wine was around in the biblical days; I know, but what about the hard liquors that are so brazenly referred to as "spirits?" Satan rarely has to hide himself these days, as we are living in a time of unimaginable darkness. When we hear the word darkness, we often think of being in a situation where we cannot see anything but black. Nevertheless, darkness refers to blindness.

Capitalism is one man's claim to fortune at the sound of another man's fall. Don't get me wrong; there is no sin in being rich, but there is a sin in being self-seeking. If GOD doesn't enrich you, you are in big trouble because your wealth will prove to eventually become a snare for your soul. Giving to the poor doesn't make a man righteous. What makes him righteous is his faith. Faith is your ability to hear and discern GOD'S voice. When you have faith, you'll know that everything that you have and all that you are belongs to GOD. In that, you will never willfully fund wars or walk by another homeless person without at least offering them a meal if you have the ability to bless them. With faith, you will not approve laws designed to remove prayer from school. With faith, you would never allow an atheist (godless man or woman) to dictate how to run a land or a home just because they pay taxes. Are we saying that money gives people the right to remove GOD from our nation? It's unfortunate that many will discover that money means nothing to a demon in hell; neither can you pay your way into Heaven. With faith, you would never turn your back on a living GOD to depend on science or any other manufactured knowledge that will prove to be worthless once you leave this earth. Yes, faith will prove to be a blessing to those who have it. It is the evidence that CHRIST lives in them, and their ticket into an everlasting paradise called Heaven.

Saints, don't link yourself up to this world's system. There is nothing godly about selfishness, nor will GOD approve man's attempt to fit in to a world who hates HIM. There isn't any amount of shouting that will justify your betrayal. *"Ye adulterers and adulteresses, know ye not that the friendship of the world is enmity with God? Whosoever therefore will be a friend of the world is the enemy of God" (James 4:4).*

Please understand that you will never be accepted by the world as a child of GOD, but you will have to reject GOD to be accepted by the world. That's one trade-off that isn't worth the paper it's written on.

Chapter 10

Systematic Slaughter of the Church

The church is being slaughtered right before our very eyes, but there aren't many who will stand up for it. As I flip through the television channels each day, I often run across stories about wicked Pastors who killed, misled, raped or robbed someone or everyone in their congregation. As the world becomes more violent and more determined to sin against the LORD, many churches are following their lead. Any church who is bold enough to stand up against sin is negatively featured throughout the media; shunned, humiliated and harassed...even by churches who side with the world against the LORD. Nowadays, many believers conceal their true beliefs out of fear of being ridiculed, or even worse, attacked. All the same, the image of the church is now being featured as an institution of hypocrites, judgmental Jezebels and thieves posing as pastors.

The truth is, there are many in the church who are wicked, and Satan sent them to discredit the church. Do you really believe Satan would frequent the club, hoping to nab one of those girls at the bar? No. That's like going inside your own refrigerator, taking what you pull out back to the store, and buying it again. Satan went to the Garden of Eden for the sole purpose of deceiving Eve. He hasn't changed. He still goes into places where GOD'S people come together with the sole purpose of deceiving them, and his agenda is to cause those who are attempting to get saved to flee back into the world. That's the whole purpose of the Jezebel spirit in the church. Its purpose is to discredit the church and make the world feel they are better off.

Find any babe in CHRIST who has just decided to change their life, and you'll likely hear a story about someone taking them under their wings. The person who took them in was likely from the church and probably had a position in the church. Oftentimes, a Jezebel will befriend those who are new to the church. She'll come off as a holy Prophet or Prophetess, and she'll help the person in which she is imprisoning. Suddenly, she'll become condescending towards that person, complaining about the clothes they wear to church, their choices, relationships and so on. After a while, she becomes venomous and negative towards the person she has charged herself with covering. *Don't get distracted by the "she" in reference to the Jezebel. Men can have this spirit as well, but it is more common in women.* Sometimes, she does this from the onset of their relationship. Because of her ways, many run back into the unpredictable claws of the world because the creature they'd just encountered is far more wicked than one they've seen in the club. They feel safer in the world than they do in the church! They undoubtedly came in contact with a Jezebel spirit. This is one of the ways the enemy is attacking the church.

Another attack comes through the media outlets. You'll find that the media is obsessed with false prophets, never taking the time out to express how many good churches are in existence; the media often showcases the bad ones. Many in the world justify their place in the world because they see so many negative stories about the church. All the same, when a Pastor does a marvelous deed, or an entire church gets out to help their community, this is rarely featured because it shines the church in a positive way. That's not to say that the media intentionally tries to discredit the church; it is to say that the enemy intentionally tries to discredit the church through the media. At the same time, when a person who promotes sin does a good deed, it is often glamorized by the media. That musician who promotes fornication and sings about murdering people is suddenly portrayed as a saint because they did a good deed. To add icing to the cake, right before that artist curses out everyone in the audience in song, they give praises to whom they revere as "god". Understand that the word "god" is not always synonymous with JEHOVAH; it depends on the person speaking it and who "their" god is. As believers, we know JEHOVAH is GOD, but many religions worship other entities that they refer to as "god". Therefore, when someone sends praises to "god", it's not always JEHOVAH they are speaking of. How can you worship a god that you don't serve? How can you promote one god (sin) and acknowledge another one? *"This people draweth nigh unto me with their mouth, and honoureth me with their lips; but their heart is far from me" (Matthew 15:8).*

Journalists often chase stories they believe will pay them the most money and get the most views. Sadly enough, stories about a hypocritical pastor are hot topics to those who are in the world. Go to YouTube and look at the video view count of any renowned man or woman of GOD. Then type their names in and add the word "exposed" behind it, and you'll find countless videos of people claiming to expose these televangelists. You'll notice that the "exposed" videos receive double or more views than the videos from the person who is "being exposed". That's because people are more interested in gossip and lies than they are in the message coming from GOD'S elect. That's not to say that everyone on television posing as a Pastor is good; that is to say that many of them are men and women of GOD, but the enemy seeks to destroy them by attempting to destroy their names. People buy into the lies more than they welcome the free Truth.

Finally, there is the government. The government is slowly but surely stripping the church of its power. If you pay attention, you'll see countless stories of Christian businesses whose First Amendment rights are being violated. The government is forcing Christians to bow down to their gods (the people and their money) rather than allowing us to practice what we believe. A good example is the issue that happened with Hobby Lobby. Because of new federal healthcare laws, Hobby Lobby and other Christian businesses are being forced to provide insurance coverage for contraceptives, morning-after and week-after pills. Hobby Lobby, of course, is owned by Christians. Because they are a for-profit company, they are being made to submit to secular laws rather than being granted the right to practice what they believe. *In other news, Atheists were successfully able to get prayer removed from school.* Back in 2012, a petition hit the Internet requesting signatures from people who wanted the "In GOD we trust" removed from American currency. Thankfully, it hasn't been done away with, but we know the enemy won't stop until he convinces the American government to remove GOD from everything. After he's done that, he will launch his attack against an unguarded nation.

But why should we whine about all that's happening? After all, the government is "for the people" and not for the LORD. The government is part of the world; something that is against GOD. Therefore, as Christians, why would we join ourselves to it? Why ally yourself with something that is working with the devil himself? *"You adulterous people, don't you know that friendship with the world means enmity against God? Therefore, anyone who chooses to be a friend of the world becomes an enemy of God" (James 4:4 NIV).*

What's amazing is any time a Pastor stands up for what is right and joins hands with what the LORD says, he or she is often attacked...not just by the world, but mostly by the church; a church that has now aligned itself with the world's thinking. This is a church who now backs politicians who hold back the world; a church who now thinks that anyone who doesn't vote for whatever devil they plan to vote for is against GOD. We are talking about a church who now opens its doors to sin, welcoming hip-hop and everything worldly into it; a church who now operates in the secular realm, welcoming anyone of worldly prestige to stand on its platforms and speak to a hungry people. *"Nevertheless, I have a few things against you: There are some among you who hold to the teaching of Balaam, who taught Balak to entice the Israelites to sin so that they ate food sacrificed to idols and committed sexual immorality. Likewise, you also have those who hold to the teaching of the Nicolaitans. Repent therefore! Otherwise, I will soon come to you and will fight against them with the sword of my mouth" (Revelation 2:14-16).* Why is this happening in the church? Because the enemy is trying to abort the WORD in the church and the credibility of the church. Praise be to GOD; however, there are still some who have not submitted themselves to the world and its teachings. There is still a remnant alive who continue to speak what GOD spoke, even though there aren't a lot of people who want to hear it. *"Yet I have left me seven thousand in Israel, all the knees which have not bowed unto Baal, and every mouth which hath not kissed him" (1 Kings 19:18).*

The systematic slaughter of the church is now in effect, but at the same time, GOD is still Sovereign and Almighty. This means that the battle is HIS and it's already won. Right now, what we see manifesting before us is the revealing of what is and what is not holy. It is the separation of who is for CHRIST and who is against HIM. Those who are for HIM will continue to speak right things, even after being persecuted, shunned and made a public spectacle of. Those who are against HIM will continue to speak as if they are for HIM, but their deeds will find them out. *"Beware of false prophets, which come to you in sheep's clothing, but inwardly they are ravening wolves. **Ye shall know them by their fruits.** Do men gather grapes of thorns, or figs of thistles? Even so every **good tree bringeth forth good fruit**; but **a corrupt tree bringeth forth evil fruit**. **A Good Tree Cannot Bring Forth Evil Fruit, Neither Can A Corrupt Tree Bring Forth Good Fruit.** Every tree that bringeth not forth good fruit is hewn down, and cast into the fire. **Wherefore by their fruits ye shall know them**"* (Matthew 7:15-20).

People of GOD, you can NEVER be for someone who is against GOD....NEVER. If you align yourself with their iniquities, you will share in their punishments.

Chapter 11

<u>Is the Modern Church Ahab'ed?</u>

"And the king of Israel and Jehoshaphat the king of Judah sat each on his throne, having put on their robes, in a void place in the entrance of the gate of Samaria; and all the prophets prophesied before them" (2 Chronicles 18:10).

Ahab was once a man of GOD, but he went against the LORD and married a Phoenician woman named Jezebel. She was the daughter of a King; a pagan who practiced Baal worship. GOD forewarned Ahab not to marry Jezebel or any woman who was not an Israelite, but he did not listen. Ahab was king of North Israel, and by marrying a Phoenician woman, he was allying himself with Phoenicia and all of its practices. This was very common in those days when one kingdom feared another one or wanted to unite with another kingdom to become stronger. Weaker kingdoms would seek out protection from larger kingdoms by intermarrying their sons with their daughters. This exchange also meant the weaker kingdom would take on the beliefs of the stronger one. Ahab's decision to marry Jezebel was done out of rebellion, fear and lust. He rebelled against GOD by disobeying HIM; he feared Phoenicia so he acted upon that fear, and he lusted after the strange women that Phoenicia had to offer.

After marrying Jezebel, Ahab turned on GOD

and begin to worship Baal; Jezebel's god. In doing so, he caused Israel to sin because he was the king of North Israel; therefore, whatever god he served would have to be served by the people.

Because of Ahab's decision to marry Jezebel, he became one of the most wicked men ever mentioned in the Bible. He sat by and allowed his wife to murder the Prophets of a GOD he once served. He allowed his wife to write decrees in his name; he allowed his wife to emasculate him. Isn't this what many of the churches are doing today? Out of fear, many align themselves with the world and its doctrine. They intermarry their daughters and sons with the sons and daughters of the world. They criticize, shun and oppose GOD'S true Prophets, even publicly denouncing truths spoken by men and women of GOD. They open new churches surrounded by yellow ribbon that they give Jezebel the honor of cutting. They open the doors of the church and welcome all manner of men and women inside, but this is not the sin. The sin is many ordain broken and dark souls, giving them the keys and permission to mislead GOD'S people into sin and sexual immorality. The world says fornication is good, and many in the church agreed. The world says same sex unions are good, and many in the church are now folding under the pressure to accept this way of thinking. "Judge ye not" is becoming the new American church motto, as many have given themselves to the ways and mindsets of the world.

*"Nevertheless, I have this against you: You tolerate that woman Jezebel, who calls herself a prophet. By her teaching she misleads **my servants** into sexual immorality and the eating of food sacrificed to idols. I have given her*

time to repent of her immorality, but she is
unwilling. So I will cast her on a bed of
suffering, and I will make those who **commit**
adultery with her *suffer intensely,* **unless**
they repent of her ways. *I will strike her*
children dead. Then **all the churches** *will*
know that I am he who searches hearts and
minds, and I will repay each of you according
to your deeds.

Now I say to the rest of you in Thyatira, to you
who do not hold to **her teaching** *and have not*
learned **Satan's so-called deep secrets**, *'I will*
not impose any other burden on you, except to
hold on to what you have until I come'"
(Revelation 2:20-25 NIV).

There are a few points that I highlighted
because I wanted to elaborate more on them.

"By her teaching she misleads my servants." Why does the LORD say that she

is misleading HIS servants? Understand that

Satan leads his own, but he misleads the

people of GOD. How is this done? By deceiving them into believing that they are following CHRIST, when in truth, they are following Baal. CHRIST made it clear that the teachings are "her teachings" and not HIS own.

"I will make those who commit adultery with her suffer intensely, unless they repent of her ways." Why is it being referred to as adultery? GOD calls HIS people HIS bride; therefore, when a believer submits to another authority, they are committing idolatry against the LORD. Idolatry is the same as adultery; only in a spiritual sense. HE also made it clear that those ways (acts and beliefs) were her (Jezebel's) ways. Remember, Jezebel hated GOD, but she was a worshipper of the flesh. Whatever the flesh wanted; the flesh was granted. She killed and persecuted the Prophets of GOD. In the world's system, this is still being done. People submit to the lusts of their flesh, and the government is being

182

pressured to put away GOD and marry Baal. Therefore, if you are a believer and you find yourself participating in the world's system, you have joined yourself to the devil.

"Then all the churches will know that I am he who searches hearts and minds." What's amazing about this line is that the LORD is making it very clear that all churches are not of HIM. Every church that claims CHRIST is not of or for HIM. Many of them don't understand or know that it is HE who searches the hearts and minds of the people. Can you imagine being in a church of unbelievers being taught to believe upon a GOD that the leaders themselves are unsure of?

"Now I say to the rest of you in Thyatira, to you who do not hold to her teaching and have not learned Satan's so-called deep secrets...." Here, we learn that there is a remnant of GOD, and there will continue to be a remnant who does not bow to Baal. "Her teaching" refers to the teachings of Jezebel, and Jezebel teaches Baal worship. Again, Baal worship refers to flesh worship, amongst other forms of worship. Even though GOD says fornication is a sin, a Baal worshipper will not see a problem with fornication. Many churches don't shake their heads at fornication as long as it occurs between a man and a woman. Baal worship would agree with men being with men and women being with women because this lust is fleshly rooted. Baal worship says to give the flesh what it wants, whereas GOD warned us that the flesh wars against the spirit and the spirit against the flesh. Homosexuality is sexual immorality, but get this...so is fornication. You can never measure one sin as worse than the other; either way, a sin is an act that opposes the living GOD. The church has to stop welcoming sin.....period!

Jehoshaphat (king of Judah) was a man of GOD who aligned himself with Ahab, even though Ahab and his wife, Jezebel, were murderers of GOD'S Prophets. Nevertheless, Jehoshaphat allied with Ahab; even married his son Jehoram with Ahab's daughter Athaliah. When Ahab wanted to go up to war against Ramoth-Gilead, he asked Jehoshaphat if he would join him in this war, and he agreed to do it. First, he requested that a Prophet be consulted. Here's the story: *"Now Jehoshaphat had great wealth and honor, and he allied himself with Ahab by marriage. Some years later he went down to see Ahab in Samaria. Ahab slaughtered many sheep and cattle for him and the people with him and urged him to attack Ramoth Gilead. Ahab king of Israel asked Jehoshaphat king of Judah, "Will you go with me against Ramoth Gilead?" Jehoshaphat replied, "I am as you are, and my people as your people; we will join you in the*

185

war." But Jehoshaphat also said to the king of Israel, "First seek the counsel of the Lord."

So the king of Israel brought together the prophets—four hundred men—and asked them, "Shall we go to war against Ramoth Gilead, or shall I not?"

"Go," they answered, "for God will give it into the king's hand." But Jehoshaphat asked, "Is there no longer a prophet of the Lord here whom we can inquire of?" The king of Israel answered Jehoshaphat, "There is still one prophet through whom we can inquire of the Lord, but I hate him because he never prophesies anything good about me, but always bad. He is Micaiah son of Imlah." "The king should not say such a thing," Jehoshaphat replied" (2 Chronicles 18:1-7 NIV).

There are so many points that should be highlighted here, but we'll go on what we see.

- First, we see that Jehoshaphat had

great wealth and honor, so why is it that
he aligned himself with Ahab? The
same reason Ahab aligned himself with
Phoenicia; it was all done out of fear.
They believed in strength in numbers;
they joined what would undoubtedly
become their enemies so they wouldn't
be enemies. Again, this was common in
those days.

- Next, we see that Jehoshaphat first
  agreed to go with him and then tried to
  make it right by requesting that they
  seek the counsel of the LORD. What
  Jehoshaphat was denying himself was
  the fact that who Ahab considered his
  lord wasn't the same GOD that he
  served.

- Ahab brought together four hundred
  prophets, and not one of them was a
  prophet of the LORD. They were all
  prophets of Baal. Why under heaven

187

did he need four hundred prophets? Because false prophets lie, and Ahab wanted to get as many confirmations as he could. Yet, it took one Prophet of GOD to come in and tell him the truth, even though he didn't want it.

- Ahab showed his true heart by telling Jehoshaphat that he hated the Prophet of GOD because he prophesied evil to him, and not good. This was Jehoshaphat's door of escape, but like many today, he was too busy trying to stay on Ahab's good side that he slightly rebuked him and let it go.

- Jehoshaphat recognized that these men who came before them to prophesy were <u>not</u> prophets of GOD. So why did he stay and continue with Ahab? Fear, of course.

- Even after Micaiah (GOD'S Prophet)

warned them not to go, Jehoshaphat still
went with Ahab. He feared Ahab more
than he feared GOD.

Such are many of the churches today. They
ally themselves with the world out of fear. Pay
attention to every big event that the world
stands still for, and look at many of the
churches; they freeze too because they have
not disassociated themselves from the world.
Instead, they have joined in with the world, and
there is no way to distinguish between them
unless you specifically ask who is who.
Jezebel has struck fear in Elijah (the church)
once again, even though the church has
witnessed the power of GOD.

Unlike Ahab, however, Jehoshaphat repented.
He had a heart for GOD and never turned on
GOD, even throughout his alliance with Ahab.
His sin was that he feared Ahab and allied
himself with such a wicked man. His sin was

that he intermarried into Ahab's family, and even after seeking GOD'S counsel, he still went into war against Ramoth-Gilead with Ahab. GOD put the truth in Micaiah's (HIS Prophet) mouth, but Jehoshaphat did not hearken to what he said. What's funny is Ahab then requested that he wear his kingly attire in the war, but Ahab refused to wear his. *"So the king of Israel and Jehoshaphat king of Judah went up to Ramoth Gilead. The king of Israel said to Jehoshaphat, "I will enter the battle in disguise, but you wear your royal robes." So the king of Israel disguised himself and went into battle" (2 Chronicles 18:28-29 NIV).* Why did Ahab request that Jehoshaphat wear his royal robe while he disguised himself? Because he was trying to preserve his own life! Ahab knew that in every war, the warriors were trained to catch the king and bring him before their king. There they would kill him, or oftentimes, they will kill him during the war and take his head back to their kingdom as proof and as a trophy. In some cases, they would simply imprison the king for the rest of his life. Ahab sent Jehoshaphat in to take a dart for him, hoping that if anyone was killed, it would be Jehoshaphat and not himself. Why would Jehoshaphat think that Ahab could allow Jezebel to kill all of GOD'S Prophets and Ahab could openly say that he hated the one living Prophet of GOD (Micaiah), but that he (Jehoshaphat) would be safe as a man of GOD around Ahab? Isn't this what many believers think today? Even though they see that the world hates the church, they still join themselves with the world, and think that they are safe. Even though many see how the world persecutes the church, many join hands with the world hoping that by allying themselves with the world, they are safe from the world's hand of vengeance. They are secret Christians; people who are ashamed to call JESUS CHRIST LORD in front of a world who hates HIM. They are public sinners but private saints. What warning did CHRIST give them? *"For whosoever shall be ashamed of me and of my words, of him shall the Son of man be ashamed, when he shall come in his own glory, and in his Father's, and of the holy angels" (Luke 9:26).*

Always remember that there will be kingdoms that rise up against the WORD of GOD. They will have their strength in numbers. The majority will stand in agreement, and anyone who opposes them will be their enemy. But it is better to be an enemy of the world than it is to be an enemy of GOD. All the same, remember Ahab and Jehoshaphat. Ahab was a fearful man who linked himself to an ungodly nation for the sake of feeling protected, when all he had to do was trust in the LORD. GOD would have protected him. After all, if Abraham went up against a kingdom with only 300 trained men by his side and won, why would Ahab (or anyone, for that matter) think that GOD couldn't deliver Israel from Phoenicia? Jehoshaphat was a fearful man, but he never gave in to Baal worship. Because of this, GOD forgave him for his trespasses against HIM. He was still punished, however, but he lived to repent another day. There may have been those times when you felt pressured to fit in, but GOD did not create you to fit in; HE created you to stand out. By standing up for HIM, you are standing out with HIM. After all, HE is a peculiar GOD.

Saints, do not conform to this world. I know it's easier said than done, but it is better to be shunned by the world than it is to be shooed away from the pearly gates of Heaven. In this day and age, many are being led to believe that any talk about heaven and hell is "religious folklore," but the truth is: CHRIST lives. Every knee shall bow and every tongue shall confess that HE is LORD. Wouldn't you rather confess it now than wish you could confess it later? Don't follow the majority! JESUS warned us in Matthews 7:13-14: *"Enter in at the narrow gate: for **wide is the gate**, and broad is the way, that leads to destruction, and **many there be who go in there**: Because **narrow is the gate**, and narrow is the way, which leads unto life, and **few there be that find it." (NIV)**

Chapter 12

Tares Arrayed in Priestly Garments

"Another parable put he forth unto them, saying, The kingdom of heaven is likened unto a man which sowed good seed in his field: But while men slept, his enemy came and sowed tares among the wheat, and went his way. But when the blade was sprung up, and brought forth fruit, then appeared the tares also. So the servants of the householder came and said unto him, Sir, didst not thou sow good seed in thy field? From whence then hath it tares? He said unto them, An enemy hath done this. The servants said unto him, Wilt thou then that we

go and gather them up? But he said, Nay; lest while ye gather up the tares, ye root up also the wheat with them. Let both grow together until the harvest: and in the time of harvest I will say to the reapers, Gather ye together first the tares, and bind them in bundles to burn them: but gather the wheat into my barn" (Matthew 13:24-30).

The wheat represents the believers, and the tares represent the ungodly. From the parable, we can gather that there was a mixing of the believers and the unbelievers. The LORD has committed to separating those who belong to HIM from those who do not belong to HIM. We all probably get that part, but how are the believers and unbelievers mixed in together? Where has this taken place?

America is a country known as a mixing pot,

not just because of its various races, but because of the various beliefs of the people who live here. Every religion, every cult and every devil imaginable can be found on American soil. So is America that field the LORD spoke of? No. That field is the entire world. Whatever we do in America is often mimicked throughout the earth. We are considered a great nation, hated or loved wherever we go; nevertheless, many nations follow the lead of America. Therefore, it can be said that many nations are now lands that hold both believers and unbelievers. There are some nations, however, where there are no believers in existence because they are forced to submit to the religion of that land. Then again, there are nations like Pakistan and other Islamic countries where the majority of the people are Muslim and a handful are Christian. In many of those countries, Christians are persecuted and slaughtered. What's amazing is many of those who paid for their beliefs with their lives did not give in and confess the Muslim religion. Many of them were given the chance to renounce CHRIST, but they did no such thing. Undoubtedly, GOD will reward them greatly for their perseverance and love. HE will give them everlasting life with HIM, and there is no greater reward than to be with HIM forevermore.

But let's head back to America. This is a country where many believers are afraid of being talked about to the point where they will denounce their beliefs just to fit in. All the same, there are many unbelievers posing as believers, and they are not afraid to say they love the LORD, but their actions show otherwise. Because of this, we now have many church leaders who gain the respect and trust of their congregations. They speak the truth to hungry men, women and children who desire to serve the LORD. They wear their priestly garments and appear to be holy, but time always tells what type of fruit they are really bearing. They aren't wheat; they are tares in priestly garments.

It goes without saying that many religions and churches have obviously missed the mark. How is that? GOD told us that signs and wonders would follow those who believe. In many religions and churches, there are no signs and wonders; just a bunch of people coming together on Saturday or Sunday morning to discuss their religious beliefs. After that, they dispense and go home to live life the way their religion dictated that they live. Oftentimes, they hear of signs and wonders allegedly reported in their religion, but it never happened. They never witness it because they are serving a godless religion; one that speaks of HIM but knows nothing of HIM. John 4:24

reads, *"God is a Spirit: and they that worship him must worship him in spirit and in truth."* Because GOD is a Spirit, we cannot worship HIM from the flesh. The flesh is dead, and the Bible tells us that the flesh wars against the spirit; therefore, we must worship HIM in spirit. Why is this? Galatians 5:17 explains, *"For the flesh lusteth against the Spirit, and the Spirit against the flesh: and these are contrary the one to the other: so that ye cannot do the things that ye would."* We are being warned that the flesh lusts against the spirit. This means that the flesh desires to take the place of the spirit. Our spirit is who we are; it is our life, but our flesh is simply our earthly homes. They are our permission suits to live in the realm of the earth. The flesh is dead and full of sin; that's why we had to be born again. But our spirit is what lives forever. You will find many leaders who are led by their flesh, and they are oftentimes the ones who are hungry for more followers. Their flesh not only longs to take the place of their spirit, their flesh longs to lead many people into its own version of paradise.

Because I design for ministries, I have met all types of spirits. I've met good people who truly have a heart for GOD, and I've met some dark souls whose forked tongues slipped up and revealed their heart's interest: money and power. I don't say anything, nor do I attempt to judge the person; instead, I make a mental note to pray for the lost ones so they won't continue to lead by their flesh. I know that many leaders started out with a true heart for GOD, but somehow along the way, their flesh convinced them to put their ministries in the backseat. Their flesh took the lead as they were enticed by the lusts of having mega churches, fame, power and prestige. Don't get me wrong: it is great for a man or woman of

GOD to have a huge following or a mega church, but this ought to be done in CHRIST, provided by CHRIST; it should be established to win souls, for the coming together of the saints, for teaching, reproofing, deliverance and to invite the presence of GOD amongst HIS people. When the leader's eyes are clouded with dollar signs and thoughts of huge photos of themselves, they become blinded by their own lusts. The desire should always be to grow to bless more people; that's it. The desire should be to have beautiful ministries trimmed in excellence and established by faith; nevertheless, this should not be done for the Pastor. It should be done for the people of GOD.

When a leader's heart becomes dark, and he begins to lead by his flesh, that leader becomes worse than a tare. He is not just a tare sown amongst the wheat; he is a farmer who waters his pockets and his lusts by taking from the wheat. His congregation is unknowingly following after his flesh and his lusts. Just like Ahab, he misled the people and caused them to sin. That's why we must repent for sins known and unknown. He looks for approval in the eyes of those who follow him. He listens for the applause of the congregation, and when he doesn't receive it, he becomes inwardly enraged. Like Satan, he desires the position of GOD, so he deceived many into following after him. To him, the sky is the limit. He wants to take "his" ministry to the four corners of the earth, but it's not done because he wants to see millions of souls saved. He wants to see millions of souls sitting in **his** church, sowing into **his** pockets and praising **him** from every corner. *As I mention in every book, when I say "he" or "him", I mean both men and women.* Anyone who dares to oppose his flesh is met by harsh words, followed by even more wicked prayers and false prophesies. He desires the fall of anyone who preaches the uncompromising gospel of JESUS CHRIST. His true motives are revealed when he is given the chance to be seated amongst the rich and powerful people of the world. He will justify them and any dark words they speak. Even though they are against the LORD, he is for them. To the world, he portrays a man (or woman) who wants to see this powerful character's soul saved, but this is not the truth. Those who are powerful to the world are powerful to him because his flesh is leading him. He lusts after their power and prestige. He surrounds himself with millionaires and billionaires of all faiths. He doesn't give to the poor; he gives to the rich in hopes of drawing some of their "anointing" for wealth. The poor, to him, are nobodies. If he gives a little to the poor, he feels that he's gotten over on the LORD. He considers his own works, but not his heart. *"One who oppresses the poor to increase his wealth and one who gives gifts to the rich--both come to poverty" (Proverbs 22:16).* He knows what the Bible says about him, but he reinterprets the scriptures so that his darkness won't be found out. After all, he doesn't truly believe the scriptures. If he did, he would repent of his ways and turn back to CHRIST. Because he does not, he continues to follow after his lusts. He collects souls just as a devil does; the more he has, the more powerful he feels. When a poor man in his congregation is not present or is sick, he doesn't visit him, nor does he care for that man's health; nevertheless, when a millionaire is missing, he notices. When those who sow into him are not present, he calls to check in on them. When those who openly praise him are absent, he notices because he is deprived of his weekly praise. The poor cry out to him for help, but he turns his head.

"Whoso stoppeth his ears at the cry of the poor, he also shall cry himself, but shall not be heard" (Proverbs 21:13). The wealthy call him, and they have his "special" phone number. He justifies his lusts by misquoting the scriptures; not understanding that GOD doesn't just look upon the deeds of a man; GOD looks at his heart. Our hearts are our faces to GOD. A man's deeds only bear witness to what is in his heart. A man's deeds can be deceiving, for a self-serving man could do something nice or heroic and still be a dark and twisted soul. If you've lived long enough, you have had friends that have proven this theory to be true. *"Woe be unto the pastors that destroy and scatter the sheep of my pasture! saith the LORD. Therefore thus saith the LORD God of Israel against the pastors that feed my people; Ye have scattered my flock, and driven them away, and have not visited them: behold, I will visit upon you the evil of your doings, saith the*

LORD. And I will gather the remnant of my flock out of all countries whither I have driven them, and will bring them again to their folds; and they shall be fruitful and increase. And I will set up shepherds over them which shall feed them: and they shall fear no more, nor be dismayed, neither shall they be lacking, saith the LORD" (Jeremiah 21:3-4).

There are many dark souls clothed in priestly apparel. Don't look at what they are wearing on the outside; pay attention to their fruit. Their fruit will bear witness to the types of seeds that are growing in their hearts. In this hour, there are many who are misleading the people of GOD, but the error isn't just in those leaders; the error is in the people who follow them. *"My sheep hear my voice, and I know them, and they follow me: And I give unto them eternal life; and they shall never perish, neither shall any man pluck them out of my hand" (John*

10:27-28). To know HIS voice, you must have a personal relationship with HIM. Too many people are depending on their Pastor's relationships with the LORD rather than having their own. This undoubtedly has caused many people to be deceived, because when we have faith in GOD, we have the substance needed to keep us from following empty vessels. To get this faith, we must hear the WORD of GOD. *"So then faith cometh by hearing, and hearing by the word of God" (Romans 10:17).* How can you hear the WORD? Read it. You hear with your ears and you hear with your heart. Read it silently or read it aloud. People who read the Bible only at church, and people who only pray to GOD on Sundays, are not worshippers of the living GOD; they are worshippers of their Pastors and worshippers of Sunday. They worship the day, reverence the church building, and honor their own understandings. JEHOVAH is the GOD of everyday! All the same, we (believers) are the actual temples of the HOLY SPIRIT! Therefore, it's not the church building that is holy; it's the people in it who are holy. The buildings had to be sanctified in the olden days before the death and resurrection of CHRIST, and only the Levites and Priests could enter. Of course, they had to be consecrated through ritualistic acts of sacrificing lambs and goats, but we have the Blood of JESUS. We don't need the sacrifice of animals anymore; CHRIST gave HIS life for us, and now we are under grace. We are no longer under the Mosaic law; therefore, we are now holy because GOD inhabits us! When you leave the church building, HE comes with you. When you sin, HE is right there witnessing your act! HE doesn't wait for you on Sunday morning to show up at the church building; HE comes there with you. HE said HE would never leave nor forsake you, and HE meant it.

The next time you decide to join or visit to a new church, make sure you pray about it first. Seek GOD so that you don't end up being misled by a leader who sees you as just another number to count amongst his followers. Always ask the LORD to send you to be fed by Pastors who love and fear HIM. Make sure the leader is one who was sent by GOD. *"And I will give you pastors according to mine heart, which shall feed you with knowledge and understanding" (Jeremiah 3:15).*

Chapter 13

<u>Human Branding</u>

Over the years, the branding of human beings
has been commonplace in many countries. It
is believed to have originated as punishment to
runaway slaves and criminals. Of course, at
that time, no one wanted to be branded; it
served as a double punishment: it was painful,
and secondly, it was humiliating. Slave owners
oftentimes branded their slaves so they could
be identified as their personal property. In
ancient Rome, fugitive slaves were labeled
with the letters FUG, which; of course, stands
for fugitive. The original intention of branding a
person is to leave a distinctive mark that is

permanent. This mark would identify the offense committed by the person who had been branded, or it would identify who the person was the property of.

When human branding made its way to Britain, it was then used as by the Anglo-Saxons. Under the Statute of Vagabonds, anyone considered to be a vagabond or Gypsy would be branded with a large V on their chests. In the days of slavery, people were often branded on their faces so the mark could easily be seen. Human branding slowly made its way into the church, first being used in the 16th century as punishment to Anabaptists who refused to join the Roman Catholic Church.

Fast forward to today. Many of the laws that allowed for human branding have now been repealed. When slavery was abolished in America, many of the slaves were offered wage-slavery. The slave-master would offer to pay them minimum wages in return for their service. Everything pretty much would remain the same, but the slave would now be considered a hired worker, and was no longer to be treated as property. Many slaves accepted this agreement, while others fled north. Wage-slavery is basically the exchange of money for service or to pay off a debt. In wage-slavery, the servant was underpaid, and it would often take years before the servant could buy his own freedom (that is if he was working to pay off a debt). Nevertheless, he was not branded since laws that allowed for human branding had been repealed.

Nowadays, people voluntarily brand themselves with what we refer to as tattoos. Tattoos are not a new form of branding. As a matter of fact, tattoos were once used on criminals in the same way a hot or cold iron was used to brand them. In the mid 80s, tattoos were often used to express gang affiliation. The mark identified the member as a slave of a particular gang. Of course, not many would own up to the fact that they are slaves to the one who leads the gang because of pride, but placing yourself in debt to another person is slavery.

Nowadays, tattoos are used as a form of artistic expression. People often get tattoos to represent anything from a group, a loved one or whatever they are into. American culture has tried to redefine the meaning of a tattoo, and even though some of today's socially elite have tattoos; tattoos are mainly found in working class to impoverished areas and amongst the youth. Professionals with tattoos often get their bodies inked in places that they can easily cover up when going into a professional environment. With today's youth and in some poorer areas, you will find that the tattoos are more visible. All the same, how class is defined in modern society is by social-economic wealth, when in truth, a wealthy man can have the mindset of poverty. He may have inherited his wealth, or he may have earned his wealth by targeting products or services to working-class Americans. You can find some people who live slightly above or below the poverty line, but their mindset is one of wealth. Give them a little time, and their financial situation will catch up with their mindset.

But how does GOD feel about us marking up our bodies? It's simple: HE doesn't like it. Here are a few scriptures which confirms this:

- **Leviticus 19:28**- *"Ye shall not make any cuttings in your flesh for the dead, nor print any marks upon you: I am the LORD."*

- **1 Corinthians 6:19-20**- *"What? Know*

215

ye not that your body is the temple of the Holy Ghost which is in you, which ye have of God, and ye are not your own? For ye are bought with a price: therefore glorify God in your body, and in your spirit, which are God's."

- **Romans 12:1**- *"I beseech you therefore, brethren, by the mercies of God, that ye present your bodies a living sacrifice, holy, acceptable unto God, which is your reasonable service."*

Understand that as HIS temple, you are holy. Would you buy a church and spray graffiti on it? You are holier than any physical building put together by man's hands, for you were put together by GOD and made in HIS likeness. Would you buy a brand new Rolls Royce and then carve your name on it? Of course not! You are far more valuable than a Rolls Royce or anything created by man; you are GOD-created. Tattoos often represent that the person wearing them is or was a slave to a certain mindset, despite their social-economic status. GOD doesn't want us to walk around enslaved to any mentality or chained into any lifestyle. *"For ye are bought with a price: therefore glorify God in your body, and in your spirit, which are God's" (1 Corinthians 6:20).* Your decisions today will determine what doors open for you, and what doors close in your face tomorrow. Understand that your way of thinking today won't necessarily be your way of thinking tomorrow. People often mark the times of their lives when they are having the most fun or the most agony. In doing so, they put a leash on themselves where they can never go too far outside of that time because the marks on their bodies serve as constant reminders of where they've been. GOD gave us a memory for that. It goes without saying, if you are having a good time, you may want to stay there; howbeit, there are better times to come if you'll only keep living and serving the LORD. All the same, when someone passes that you love, you may want to honor them by marking yourself, but this is no honor to them. This is a dishonor to GOD, since HIS SPIRIT inhabits you. Let's read Leviticus 19:28 again. *"Ye shall not make any cuttings in your flesh for the dead, nor print any marks upon you: I am the LORD."* You should never honor the dead; you honor the living! How so? CHRIST paid the price, so when a believer passes away from his or her body; they are not to be mourned. After all, they are going to live forever with the LORD; nevertheless, when an unbeliever passes, that's another story.

- *"A good name is better than fine perfume, and the day of death better than the day of birth" (Ecclesiastes 7:1 NIV).*

- *"Precious in the sight of the LORD is the death of his saints" (Psalms 116:15).*

You should never represent death in any fashion, for death is an enemy of GOD. *"The last enemy to be destroyed is death" (1 Corinthians 15:26).* Sure, we mourn because we know we will miss them, and we hate to part ways with them; nevertheless, a believer dies only once, but he rises again in CHRIST. An unbeliever dies twice: the death of the flesh and the second death, which is being thrown into the lake of fire that burns forevermore.

I marked my body when I was 17 or 18-years-old. I didn't yet understand that my mind would change one day. I thought I would just get better as I was; therefore, I had the word "scandalous" tattooed on my arm. *(Sadly enough, I thought I'd get even more scandalous because I was in the world at that time, and I saw my ways as good).* It represented my "then" way of thinking, and it represented how I wanted to be seen. Nowadays, as a new creature in CHRIST, I am no longer "scandalous", even though the tattoo remains. I do plan to have it removed one day, but I use it now to minister to others who are considering a tattoo; even believers! Oftentimes, believers believe that because they are saved, their minds will not change anymore, and this is not true. GOD is constantly renewing our minds! That's why you will find some worldly saints who are simply babes in CHRIST! They are not unbelievers; they are believers who are still transitioning into holiness. They still walk like the world, act like the world and live like the world. Just give them time, and if they stay in CHRIST, their minds will change. It doesn't matter how old you get in CHRIST; your mind will continually be renewed, and you'll keep putting off the old man to embrace a whole new way of thinking. What you are doing is becoming more like GOD. If you put on a mindset and refuse to let GOD renew your mind, you are in the same rebelling against GOD. HE desires to remove that old way of thinking so you and I will be better representatives of HIM.

Your body is holy to GOD. You must treat it better than you treat your most precious material things. Understand once again that how you think today is not how you will be thinking as you grow older in CHRIST. It doesn't matter where you are in HIM; you are scheduled to grow.

- **Ephesians 4:22-24**- *"That ye put off concerning the former conversation the old man, which is corrupt according to the deceitful lusts; And be renewed in* *the spirit of your mind; And that ye put on the new man, which after God is created in righteousness and true holiness."*

- **Romans 12:2**- *"And be not conformed to this world: but be ye transformed by the renewing of your mind, that ye may prove what is that good, and acceptable, and perfect, will of God."*

- **Ezekiel 36:26**- *"A new heart also will I give you, and a new spirit will I put within you: and I will take away the stony heart out of your flesh, and I will give you an heart of flesh."*

You will never see a slave come forward to represent a free man. When you see someone on a stage holding a microphone, puffed up, tattooed and screaming at the audience; he didn't come to represent freedom; he represents bondage. That's why those who follow him will often channel whatever he is channeling. They'll let their pants sag low; they'll walk about the earth with a proud look; they'll go forth as representatives of bondage, and they will tattoo themselves to show what and who they represent. They ink themselves to represent the mindsets they are in bondage to. They will then gather followers for that mindset, souls who will now bind themselves and become slaves to that way of thinking. All the same, when you see a person on a movie acting out a fornication scene or a violent scene, they are representatives of bondage; they've come to glorify the act in which they are portraying. You will often see these characters inked up and boastful because we are all representatives of something or someone. Everyone alive is either a representative of light or a representative of darkness. If what they are presenting is against the WORD of

GOD; they are representing the enemy.
Tattoos don't represent GOD since HE told us
not to get them. Tattoos represent bondage,
and there is no way around it.

A slave was not a free man; neither was a
criminal, but you are free. You are no longer
slaves of sin or slaves of man (*unless you go
into debt*). Represent your freedom, not your
captivity. *"Wherefore he saith, When he
ascended up on high, he led captivity captive,
and gave gifts unto men" (Ephesians 4:8).*

Chapter 14

Your Role Here or Your Role There

You have an assignment from GOD, and you have an assignment from the enemy of GOD. When you serve the LORD, you will follow through to finish your assignment; when you are led by Satan, sin will follow through and finish you. *"For the wages of sin is death; but the gift of God is eternal life through Jesus Christ our Lord" (Romans 6:23).* GOD called us healed through CHRIST JESUS; this isn't just a blessing; it is an assignment. Your faith will make you whole again. GOD said we are able (through CHRIST) to tread upon serpents and scorpions, and nothing shall by any means harm us. This isn't just a blessing; it is an assignment that can only be graded by your faith in HIM. GOD gave us a sound mind; this isn't just a blessing; it is an assignment. You have to believe what HE said to rest in HIS promises. GOD said that you can say to a mountain to be removed and be cast into the sea, and it shall obey you. Should you go around moving mountains? Yes. Any mountain that stands before you is an obstacle, and your faith has the power to move it, or your fear has the power to move you. Mountains represent obstacles. In CHRIST, you aren't just blessed because you say you are; you are blessed because HE said you are. If you are in bondage and walking about as a curse, you are operating against HIS command for you, for you aren't just blessed because you want to be; you are blessed because you have to be. It is a command, but you can only walk in the blessings when you stand on faith. *"But without faith it is impossible to please him: for he that cometh to God must believe that he is, and that he is a rewarder of them that diligently seek him" (Hebrews 11:6).*

In the earth realm, you have an assignment, and you have a role in the lives of the people you come in contact with. With some people, your only assignment is to encourage a smile to brighten their day. With others, you are assigned to encourage them or be that light they need to find CHRIST. You come forward as a representative of CHRIST; therefore, you must walk and live in the blessings before you can convince someone else that GOD is a rewarder of those who diligently seek HIM.

America has ambassadors in many countries.

Could you imagine the ambassadors of such a powerful nation being sent to another country wearing rags and in poor health? Could you imagine America sending forth an ambassador to another nation and then imprisoning him in that country? This wouldn't happen because America wants to represent its power, wealth and beliefs; therefore, when it sends someone to another country, they will look powerful; they will have wealth, and they will speak of what America believes.

You are a Kingdom Ambassador sent forth to represent the Kingdom of GOD. How are you representing HIM? Can someone discern that you are a believer when they see you? Does your speech line up with CHRIST, or do you keep them guessing? Understand that you cannot properly represent the Kingdom of GOD in a worldly way. You either radiate holiness, or you radiate worldliness. Holiness is the very nature of GOD; worldliness represents the sin nature of man and the lies that Satan told them.

When you were in the world, you had a role in the world. People saw you a certain way; they identified you by your ways. For example, you may have known someone in the world who was known to be remarkably cruel but funny at the same time. Their cruelty was the very thing that made them funny, and people were attracted to them because they had no moral limitations. They would say whatever their wicked hearts conjured up. Even the cruelest of man had nothing on them, because they absolutely had no boundaries. Now, if you see that person in the church, you will likely expect them to be the same way. When they come off as a changed creature, you won't know how to address them or deal with them. Instead, you'll keep reminding them of how they were, because you know nothing about how they are. Many of their friends will have abandoned them because they are no longer the simple characters they once knew; they are new creatures in CHRIST, and the old man of who they were has passed away. When we enter friendships with people, we are assigned a role in their lives, and we assign them to certain roles in our lives. When people welcome you as a crazy man, for example, you can never be both sane and welcomed by them at the same time. Instead, you would have to remain in their lives as their "crazy" friend; otherwise, you'd lose their friendship.

In this life, you are operating in an assignment. If you are not in GOD'S will for your life, you are in Satan's will for your life. The world would easily hand you an assignment, and you could do pretty well at and in it; nevertheless, your blessing is found in doing the will of GOD.

There are many people who have subjected themselves to this world's system, and they have taken on new roles to fill in this earth. They don't know who they are in CHRIST; therefore, they accept the identities that the world has given them. Because they are busy in the world, they often feel accomplished; yet, they feel empty. They need the LORD, but they don't understand that the void in their lives bears witness to the distance between them and the FATHER. They seek ways to fill this void, but nothing works. Their relationships fail; counselors can't help them, and no one seems to know what to tell them. The truth is they need JESUS, and they need to get into HIS will for their lives. His will isn't just what HE wants us to do; HIS will is HIS inheritance for us. A will, in the natural, is a legal document that details what the giver of the will has left as an inheritance to the person listed as the inheritor. Therefore, HIS will for us is

HIS already declared blessings for us. What did HE leave for us in HIS will?

- **John 10:10**- *"The thief cometh not, but for to steal, and to kill, and to destroy: **I am come that they might have life, and that they might have it more abundantly**."*

- **Isaiah 53:5**- *"But he was wounded for our transgressions, he was bruised for our iniquities: the chastisement of our peace was upon him; and **with his stripes we are healed**."*

- **1 Peter 1:3-5**- *"Blessed be the God and Father of our Lord Jesus Christ, which according to his abundant mercy hath **begotten us again** unto a lively hope by the resurrection of Jesus Christ from the dead, **To an inheritance incorruptible, and undefiled, and that fadeth not away, reserved in heaven for you, Who are kept by the power of**

God through faith unto salvation ready to be revealed in the last time."

- **Luke 10:19-** *"Behold,* **I give unto you power to tread on serpents and scorpions, and over all the power of the enemy: and nothing shall by any means hurt you**."

- **1 Peter 1:2-** *"Elect according to the foreknowledge of God the Father, through sanctification of the Spirit, unto obedience and sprinkling of the blood of Jesus Christ:* **Grace unto you, and peace, be multiplied**."

- **John 3:36-** **"He that believeth on the Son hath everlasting life**: *and he that believeth not the Son shall not see life; but the wrath of God abideth on him."*

- **Matthew 10:8-** **"Heal the sick, cleanse the lepers, raise the dead, cast out devils**: *freely ye have received, freely give."*

He wills for us to rest in HIS finished works. We are simply to reap the fruit of healed; not healing, abundance; not barely getting by, a sound mind; not begging for peace to be still. We are to live under the grace of GOD, knowing that the peace of GOD is in us, and we can be confident that we have hope everlasting with the FATHER through the SON. HIS will for you and me is the roles HE has assigned us to; nevertheless, we are offered two roles: one from the LORD and one from the enemy. Whichever role we accept is the one we will finish or the one that will finish or complete us.

Chapter 15

Principalities & Devils

There are several spirits that believers need to be aware of in this system. Spirits come in the form of:

The Devil- The Devil, of course, is Satan otherwise known as Lucifer. Satan has many names, but just what are his "ranking" names?:

- *"Wherein in time past ye walked according to the course of this world, according to the **prince of the power of the air**, the spirit that now worketh in the children of disobedience..." (Ephesians 2:2).*

- *"Now is the judgment of this world: now shall the **prince of this world** be cast out" (John 12:31).*

Principal demons or principalities/ AKA Demon Prince- Ruler spirits. These are the highest ranking (under Satan himself) and will have several orders of demonic spirits and devils under them. Principalities often rule over countries, nations and territories. They operate in the heavens (not Heaven) and rule every devil under the heavens.

- *"But the **prince of the kingdom of Persia** withstood me one and twenty days: but, lo, Michael, one of the chief princes, came to help me; and I remained there with the kings of Persia" (Daniel 10:13).*
- *"Then said he, Knowest thou wherefore I come unto thee? And now will I return to fight with the **prince of Persia**: and*

236

*when I am gone forth, lo, the **prince of Grecia** shall come" (Daniel 10:20).*

- *"But when the Pharisees heard it, they said, This fellow doth not cast out devils, but by **Beelzebub** the **prince of the devils**" (Matthew 12:24).*

Powers- Powers are directly under principalities. They are assigned to carry out whatever assignments they are given by the principalities that rule them. Powers transport assignments from the realm of the heavens to the realm of the earth.

- *"Men's hearts failing them for fear, and for looking after those things which are coming on the earth: for the **powers of heaven** shall be shaken" (Luke 21:26).*

- *"For we wrestle not against flesh and blood, but against **principalities, against powers**, against the rulers of the darkness of this world, against*

spiritual wickedness in high places"
(Ephesians 6:12).

Devils/ Demons Governing spirits; they are directly under principalities and powers. There are "devils," and there is the Devil himself, whose name is Satan. Devils often inhabit or possess people. They are terrestrial spirits, meaning they rule in the realm of the earth. Unlike principalities, they cannot rule over nations; instead, they rule people. All the same, the term "devils" and "demons" can be used interchangeably. In the King James Version of the Bible, the words "demon" or "demons" are never used; instead the correct term used is "devils". Devils are fallen angels.

- *"But I say, that the things which the Gentiles sacrifice, **they sacrifice to devils**, and not to God: and I would not that ye should have fellowship with devils. Ye cannot drink the cup of the*

Lord, and the cup of devils: ye cannot be partakers of the Lord's table, and of the table of devils" (1 Corinthians 10:20-21).

- "Then he called his twelve disciples together, and gave them power and authority over **all devils**, and to cure diseases" (Luke 9:1).
- "Thou believest that there is one God; thou doest well: the **devils also believe**, and tremble" (James 2:9).
- "And certain women, which had been healed of evil spirits and infirmities, Mary called Magdalene, out of whom went **seven devils**..." (Luke 7:2).
- "And these signs shall follow them that believe; In my name shall they **cast out devils**; they shall speak with new tongues; They shall take up serpents; and if they drink any deadly thing, it shall not hurt them; they shall lay hands

> *on the sick, and they shall recover"*
> *(Mark 16:17-18).*

- *"And his fame went throughout all Syria: and they brought unto him all sick people that were taken with divers diseases and torments, and those which were possessed with devils, and those which were lunatick, and those that had the palsy; and he healed them"* *(Matthew 4:24).*

Beelzebub is a name used to refer to a principality. It was and is the name often thought of to be Satan, but Beelzebub is not Satan. Beelzebub is "Baalzebub," the principal demon of Baal worship. It is the authoring demon of this world's system; the system that Jezebel operates under. "Ba'al Zəbûb" means "lord of the heavenly dwelling".

Beelzebub was initially a principality that the

Phoenicians worshipped under, but when Ahab married Jezebel, he submitted himself to the principality (Baalzebub) that her father's kingdom had been worshipping under. They were worshipping a devil referred to as Baal, but Baal was not the principal demon himself. Baal was the "terrestrial" or "inhabiting" spirit that lived in and amongst Phoenicia. When Ahab submitted and began to worship Baal, he caused the majority of Israel (GOD'S people) to submit to Baal. In doing so, the principality Beelzebub was invited to rule over Israel. This is how Beelzebub started its rule over many of GOD'S people.

Before this, Beelzebub had found his way over Israel through King Solomon. King Solomon, in his old age, turned on GOD and began to worship the gods of his wives. One of those devils was the goddess Ashtoreth. Ashtoreth was a devil that was worshipped in other parts of Phoenicia. This means that Ashtoreth was under the order of Beelzebub, the governing principality. He also worshipped Milcom, which was another devil that ruled over the people of Phoenicia. Of all of the gods (devils) that Solomon worshipped, Ashtoreth (aka Astarte) and Milcom (aka Moloch) were specifically mentioned. *"But king Solomon loved many strange women, together with the daughter of Pharaoh, women of the Moabites, Ammonites, Edomites, Zidonians, and Hittites; Of the nations concerning which the LORD said unto the children of Israel, Ye shall not go in to them, neither shall they come in unto you: for surely they will turn away your heart after their gods: Solomon clave unto these in love. And he had seven hundred wives, princesses, and three hundred concubines: and his wives turned away his heart. For it came to pass, when Solomon was old, that his wives turned away his heart after other gods: and his heart was not perfect with the LORD his God, as was the heart of David his father. For Solomon went after Ashtoreth the goddess of the Zidonians, and after Milcom the abomination of the Ammonites" (1 King 11:1-5).*

The mention of Ashtoreth (Asherah) is especially important because it will help you to better understand how that devil has made its way into Christian practices today. Ashtoreth (Asherah) is also known as Ishtar, the goddess of fertility. Ashtoreth (Asherah) was the goddess that the Egyptians worshipped. The sphinx, lion, dove and other symbols were used to represent Ashtoreth (Asherah) in Middle Eastern religions. Ashtoreth (Asherah) is also known as the "evening star". Ishtar (Ashtoreth/ Asherah) was worshipped in several Assyrian cities, and was considered the goddess of sexuality, fertility, war and love. Ishtar was worshipped in many pagan religions and was eventually called "Easter" by many English-speaking nations. Asherah (Ashtoreth/Ishtar) was believed to be the mother of Baal and considered the Babylonian goddess of the sea.

As we discussed earlier, Constantine brought Christianity to Rome, but the people were pagans and wanted no part of Christianity. To relax the people, Constantine allowed some of their pagan practices into the church. Ishtar was allowed in and called Easter. In Ishtar worship, the egg represented fertility. The Resurrection of CHRIST was renamed "Easter", and many of the pagan practices were incorporated. For example, the decorating of the eggs was done by pagans and given to families to promote fertility.

It is also believed that the name "Easter" comes from the worship of the pagan goddess

Ēostre (Ostara). Ēostre was an old Germanic goddess said to also be the goddess of fertility and the goddess of Spring. Hares and rabbits were also symbols used to represent fertility, since they are considered extremely fertile creatures. This is where the "Easter bunny" comes from. Have you ever asked yourself how does a rabbit laying eggs fit into the death and resurrection of CHRIST? It doesn't, but in changing the name of the goddess (slightly) and introducing it to Christian religion, Satan was able to get Christians to worship a devil unknowingly! *"My people are destroyed for lack of knowledge: because thou hast rejected knowledge, I will also reject thee, that thou shalt be no priest to me: seeing thou hast forgotten the law of thy God, I will also forget thy children" (Hosea 4:6).* Ēostre is also celebrated in the month of April.

According to New Advent (the Catholic

Dictionary), the practice of Easter is as follows: *"The English term, according to the Ven. Bede (De temporum ratione, I, v), relates to Estre, a **Teutonic goddess** of the **rising light of day and spring**, which deity, however, is otherwise unknown, even in the Edda (Simrock, Mythol., 362); Anglo-Saxon, eâster, eâstron; Old High German, ôstra, ôstrara, ôstrarûn; German, Ostern. April was called easter-monadh. The plural eâstron is used, because the feast lasts seven days...."* (Reference: New Advent)

As you can see, many organized religions have invited in pagan practices because they do not know or understand the origin of what they are celebrating; therefore, in celebrating Easter, you are celebrating a pagan goddess. The correct term for the resurrection of CHRIST is the Resurrection! Easter came into the Catholic Church, and now many denominations still participate in some of the practices of the

Roman Catholic Church, even though they sharply rebuke the Catholic Church. A lot of its practices can still be found in many of the Christian churches today. Religion says "follow me and ask no questions," when CHRIST said to follow HIM and try the spirits by the spirit.

Even with devils, there is a ranking system, and there are several types of demonic spirits; each recognized by its behaviors. A legion is a band of devils that has entered a person; often through failed attempts at deliverance or because someone who has been delivered returned to their sin. One devil is often referred to as an unclean spirit.

- *"And when he went forth to land, there met him out of the city a certain man, which had **devils** long time, and ware no clothes, neither abode in any house, but in the tombs. When he saw Jesus, he cried out, and fell down before him,* *and with a loud voice said, What have I to do with thee, Jesus, thou Son of God most high? I beseech thee, torment me not. (For he had commanded the unclean spirit to come out of the man. For oftentimes it had caught him: and he was kept bound with chains and in fetters; and he brake the bands, and was driven of the devil into the wilderness.) And Jesus asked him, saying, What is thy name? And he said,* **Legion***:* **because many devils were entered into him**" *(Luke 8:27-30).*

- "*And there was in their synagogue a man with* **an unclean spirit***; and he cried out, Saying, Let us alone; what have we to do with thee, thou Jesus of Nazareth? Art thou come to destroy us? I know thee who thou art, the Holy One of God. And Jesus rebuked him, saying, Hold thy peace, and come out of* him. And when **the unclean spirit** had torn him, and cried with a loud voice, he came out of him" (Mark 1:21-26).

- "When **the unclean spirit** is gone out of a man, he walketh through dry places, seeking rest; and finding none, he saith, I will return unto my house whence I came out. And when he cometh, he findeth it swept and garnished. Then goeth he, and taketh to him **seven other spirits more wicked than himself**; and they enter in, and dwell there: and the last state of that man is worse than the first " (Luke 11:24-26).

Legion simply means "multitude" or "many." Therefore, when an unclean spirit (one spirit) leaves a man, if it comes back in and finds that man put together, it will go and take with it seven more spirits more wicked than itself. This means that it will bring seven more spirits (or devils) which outrank it, and they will become what is referred to as Legion. If the man is delivered from the seven but he somehow lets them return, those seven will bring back seven more, and the numbers continue to grow. The Bible tells us that JESUS cast seven devils out of Mary Magdalene. This means HE cast out a legion of devils.

What are the rulers of darkness? They are simply high-ranking devils ruled by powers and assigned to rule over/ operate in this world's system. That's why Ephesians 6:12 refers to them as "rulers of the darkness of this world". Finally, spiritual wickedness in high places refers to powers that operate in and through people of notable rank. Let's read Ephesians 6:12 again so that we can see how GOD lists each power in order according to its rank. *"For we wrestle not against flesh and blood, but against principalities, against powers, against the rulers of the darkness of this world, against spiritual wickedness in high places" (Ephesians 6:12).*

- **Principalities**- Principal Demons/ Princes
- **Powers**- Forces Ruled by Principalities
- **Rulers of Darkness of this World**- Rulers of the World's System/ Terrestrial Devils In the Realm of the Earth
- **Spiritual Wickedness In High Places**- High ranking devils operating through people of great influence.

We needed to get a better understanding of the who's who of evil so that we will know how to free ourselves from such wickedness and to guard ourselves against demonic attacks, plots and schemes. Of course, there are many types of devils; the most common being "seducing spirits". The assignment of a

seducing spirit is to seduce a person into sin.
These are the demons that influence a man
through evil thoughts to commit adultery,
participate in fornication, murder someone, tell
lies and speak blasphemies. Their assignment
is to seduce.

- *"Now the Spirit speaketh expressly, that
  in the latter times some shall depart
  from the faith, giving heed to **seducing
  spirits**, and doctrines of devils..." (1
  Timothy 4:1).*

Seducing spirits often do the bidding of devils.
Their job is to lure the man into sin. As the
scripture above reported, they are also
assigned to lure men into submitting
themselves to the doctrines of devils. This is
the reason you will find so many religious
denominations in the earth realm today. GOD
is not a GOD of division, but of unity.
Religiousness is a divide that is designed to
confuse the people of GOD and cause many to

fall into sects or "sections" of doctrines, rather than submitting to the uncompromising and whole WORD of GOD. *"For God is not the author of confusion, but of peace, as in all churches of the saints" (1 Corinthians 14:33).* Confusion is a doctrine; that's why GOD says that HE is not the author of it.

To better understand this world's system, you have to understand who rules it. It is ruled by the enemy and all that is under him; nevertheless, CHRIST took back the authority over the earth and the heavens. Daniel prophesied of this victory in Daniel 7:27, which reads, *"And the kingdom and dominion, and the greatness of the kingdom under the whole heaven, shall be given to the people of the saints of the most High, whose kingdom is an everlasting kingdom, and all dominions shall serve and obey him."*

253

In CHRIST, we have dominion over every unclean spirit, power, principality and the rulers of darkness. In CHRIST, we are victorious because HE is victorious. *"Nay, in all these things we are **more than conquerors** through him that loved us. For I am persuaded, that neither death, nor life, nor angels, nor principalities, nor powers, nor things present, nor things to come, Nor height, nor depth, nor any other creature, shall be able to separate us from the love of God, which is in Christ Jesus our Lord" (Romans 8:37-29).* This is the reason that we are NOT to submit ourselves to a system run by wickedness, devils, powers and principalities. Instead, we stand above it all; Satan and everything under him rests under our feet. Going under this world's system is the same as going under the rule of Satan.

Other pagan rituals and acts welcomed

nowadays by modern society and the church include:

- **Horoscopes**- Horoscopes were derived as a form of divination. It was a Babylonian practice that started as early as 1800 BC. It originally came from Baal worship as well. Babylonians believed that their gods would manifest in the forms of planets and stars. *"And they left all the commandments of the Lord their God, and made them molten images, even two calves, and made a grove, and worshipped all the host of heaven, and served Baal" (2 Kings 17:16).*

- **Christmas Tree**- Trees were once worshipped by pagan Europeans, and it made its way into the celebration of CHRIST. Scandinavians used to decorate their houses with trees for the New Year to scare away devils. *"Hear* *ye the word which the L*ORD *speaketh unto you, O house of Israel: Thus saith the L*ORD*, Learn not the way of the heathen, and be not dismayed at the signs of heaven; for the heathen are dismayed at them. For the customs of the people are vain: for one cutteth a tree out of the forest, the work of the hands of the workman, with the axe. They deck it with silver and with gold; they fasten it with nails and with hammers, that it move not. They are upright as the palm tree, but speak not: they must needs be borne, because they cannot go. Be not afraid of them; for they cannot do evil, neither also is it in them to do good" (Jeremiah 10:1-5).*

- **Traditional Christmas Celebration**-
There are so many pagan beliefs and rituals that have been incorporated into Christmas; not to mention, CHRIST was

not born on December 25th. Isis (also known as the queen of heaven) was believed to have conceived a son, and this son was reported to be born on December 24th. The Babylonian name for "infant" was Yule. (Sound familiar?) The colors used to represent Yule were red and green. Reindeer are symbols used to represent the pagan god, Stag. As a matter of fact, Santa is believed to be the pagan Stag god. He is believed to be omniscient; knowing all things about everyone at all times, and omnipresent; being everywhere at one time. Saturn, a Roman deity, was honored between December 17th through December 23rd during a festival known as Saturnalia.

- **New Year's Eve Celebration**- This is also linked to the pagan god, Saturn. It is celebrated with an overwhelming presence of candles, and this celebration takes place on what is referred to as the "birthday of the Unconquerable Sun", not Son. The "Unconquerable Sun's" birthday is said to be December 25th.

- **Valentine's Day**- Cupid was believed to be the son of the Greek goddess Venus. Venus was believed to be the daughter of the Greek god Jupiter. Cupid was also called Nimrod, Osiris and Tammuz. The bow and arrow represented Babylonian beliefs that Nimrod was a mighty hunter. Valentine's day was a day to celebrate fertility; therefore, it was celebrated by drunkenness, the giving of flowers and anything sweet. It was also celebrated with orgies.

Of course, we discussed earlier that Halloween was pagan (obviously). People of GOD, what was just shared here is just scratching the surface. Most holiday celebrations in America can be traced back to pagan roots. So what's next? Many people will continue to celebrate them, and they will do like Constantine did: they will try to give these pagan practices a Christian undertone to justify celebrating it. They will argue that they have made it holy by celebrating GOD on "that" day while pagans are out worshipping their gods. In truth, we should not participate period! *"And have no fellowship with the unfruitful works of darkness, but rather reprove them" (Ephesians 5:11).* I know of many churches who celebrate Halloween and will justify the celebration; nevertheless, GOD says to have no fellowship with their works. The list above was short, but if you research what you are celebrating, you will find that **<u>MOST</u>** of it comes from the Babylonians, and most of it is directly linked to Baal/ Beelzebub. If you have ever wondered why GOD calls you to come out from under the system, you know now! It is pagan; it is the worship of devils! It is submitted to powers that are ungodly! Come out from her, people of GOD. *"How is Sheshach taken! And how is the praise of the whole earth surprised! How is Babylon become an astonishment among the nations! The sea is come up upon Babylon: she is covered with the multitude of the waves thereof. Her cities are a desolation, a dry land, and a wilderness, a land wherein no man dwelleth, neither doth any son of man pass thereby. And I will punish Bel in Babylon, and I will bring forth out of his mouth that which he hath swallowed up: and the nations shall not flow together any more unto him: yea, the wall of Babylon shall fall. My people, go ye out of the midst of her, and deliver ye every man his soul from the fierce anger of the LORD. And lest your heart faint, and ye fear for the rumour that shall be heard in the land; a rumour shall both come one year, and after that in another year shall come a rumour, and violence in the land, ruler against ruler. Therefore, behold, the days come, that I will do judgment upon the graven images of Babylon: and her whole land shall be confounded, and all her slain shall fall in the midst of her. Then the heaven and the earth, and all that is therein, shall sing for Babylon: for the spoilers shall come unto her from the north, saith the LORD. As Babylon hath caused the slain of Israel to fall, so at Babylon shall fall the slain of all the earth. Ye that have escaped the sword, go away, stand not still: remember the LORD afar off, and let Jerusalem come into your mind. We are confounded, because we have heard reproach: shame hath covered our faces: for strangers are come into the sanctuaries of the LORD'S house. Wherefore, behold, the days come, saith the LORD, that I will do judgment upon her graven images: and through all her land the wounded shall groan. Though Babylon should mount up to heaven, and though she should fortify the height of her strength, yet from me shall spoilers come unto her, saith the LORD. A sound of a cry cometh from Babylon, and great destruction from the land of the Chaldeans: Because the LORD hath spoiled Babylon, and destroyed out of her the great voice; when her waves do roar like great waters, a noise of their voice is uttered: Because the spoiler is come upon her, even upon Babylon, and her mighty men are taken, every one of their bows is broken: for the LORD God of recompences shall surely requite. And I will make drunk her princes, and her wise men, her captains, and her rulers, and her mighty men: and they shall sleep a perpetual sleep, and not wake, saith the King, whose name is the LORD of hosts. Thus saith the LORD of hosts; The broad walls of Babylon shall be utterly broken, and her high gates shall be burned with fire; and the people shall labour in vain, and the folk in the fire, and they shall be weary" (Jeremiah 51:41-58).*

Chapter 16

<u>Whores of the System</u>

There is a reason that GOD referred to believers as whoremongers when they participated in idolatry. Idolatry is spiritual adultery. We are only to be in submission to HIM, our GOD in Heaven; we should not submit to man, devils or doctrines of devils. *"For this ye know, that no whoremonger, nor unclean person, nor covetous man, who is an idolater, hath any inheritance in the kingdom of Christ and of God"* *(Ephesians 5:5).*

To be unclean means to be "tainted" or to have the presence of something that makes you impure. If a wife commits adultery against her husband, for example, she becomes impure because she will carry the soul of the other man. The man will be joined in one flesh with her, making him her husband; nevertheless, men are not carriers; they are projectors or imparters. Men impart themselves into a woman when intercourse takes place.

- *"What? Know ye not that he which is joined to an harlot is one body? For two, saith he, shall be one flesh" (1 Corinthians 6:16).*

- *"But I say unto you, That whosoever shall put away his wife, saving for the cause of fornication, causeth **her** to commit adultery: and whosoever shall marry **her** that is divorced committeth adultery" (Matthew 5:32).*

The reason the scripture says he causes "her" to commit adultery is simple but yet somewhat complicated if you don't understand soul ties.

Men of old had multiple wives because when a man joins himself to a woman, he imparts himself into her. GOD uses the natural to represent the spiritual. Because women are carriers, we become pregnant when a man imparts a seed into us, and that seed fertilizes an egg. In the times before and right after CHRIST, a wife could not remarry if her husband was still alive, even if he'd put her away. That's because the two were still one.

When Amnon raped his sister Tamar, he was out of order because he did not ask her father (his Dad, David) for her hand in marriage. In those days, it was not frowned upon for a relative to marry another relative, because the Jews wanted to keep themselves pure from intermarrying with outsiders. If you know the story, Amnon was smitten with his sister Tamar. He was so obsessed with her that he became sick (bewitched/ obsessed to the point where he couldn't function properly). Jonadab was a cousin of Amnon, and he asked Amnon why he wasn't looking so good. Amnon made it known to Jonadab that he was in love with Tamar. Jonadab told him to pretend to be sick and ask David to send Tamar to feed him. When Tamar would enter the room, Amnon was to rape her. Amnon took this wicked advice and put his plan into action. Tamar begged Amnon not to rape her. She told him to do things the right way and ask David for her hand in marriage. She told Amnon that she was confident that David would not withhold her from him, but Amnon wouldn't listen. He raped her anyway. In doing so, he became her husband illegally, and Tamar would be a disgrace amongst the people unless Amnon carried out his duties as a husband to her. At the same time, a rape did not guarantee the approval of the father to give his daughter to a man. In such cases, the woman would remain with her father until the husband passed away, or she passed away. She could never remarry (since sex was and is the uniting of two people in matrimony). She could never wear the garments of a virgin; meaning, it became public knowledge that she was not a virgin, but it also was known that no man had stepped up to cover her. (There were also garments for widows; therefore, if a woman did not wear the garments of a virgin or a widow, she was undoubtedly a wife. If there was no husband there to cover her, she was considered a whore.)

After the rape, the Bible tells us that Amnon hated Tamar and demanded that she leave his room. This act was even more wicked than the rape, because he was basically saying that he would not cover her as a husband; but just as soon as he'd married her, he was putting her away. How did Tamar respond to this? *"Then Amnon hated her exceedingly; so that the hatred wherewith he hated her was greater than the love wherewith he had loved her. And Amnon said unto her, Arise, be gone. And she said unto him, There is no cause:* **this evil in sending me away is greater than the other that thou didst unto me.** *But he would not hearken unto her. Then he called his servant that ministered unto him, and said, Put now this woman out from me, and bolt the door after her. And she had a garment of divers colours upon her: for with such robes were the king's daughters that were virgins apparelled. Then his servant brought her out, and bolted the door after her. And Tamar put ashes on her head, and rent her garment of divers colours that was on her, and laid her hand on her head, and went on crying"* (2 Samuel 13:15-19).

Why did Tamar say the act of sending her away was even more wicked than the rape

itself?

- A woman who was not a virgin was either a wife or a widow. A woman was disgraced if she had been involved sexually with a man, even if she had been raped. She would remain in her father's house all the days of her life, or until her "husband" died.

- She would be a public disgrace and would be shunned by all that saw her.

- As a warning to men, she could not wear the garments of a virgin or a widow. Her attire warned men that she was not available.

- If her rape story wasn't believed, she could possibly be stoned to death.

- Tamar was a princess; she would be a famous, but public, disgrace to her people.

- There was a possibility that she would never have children or live together with

271

a man as a wife, because no Jewish man would marry her because of their customs.

- If she was ever to marry, she would be labeled a whore.

Why did Tamar rip her garment of diverse colors?

- She was no longer a virgin. The garment she was wearing was the garment of a virgin. It was against the law for a woman who was not a virgin to wear the garments of a virgin.

- To protest the act that was done to her. This signified that she had been raped by all who saw her. A woman who knowingly was about to become a wife would bring along wifely garments, but a woman who had been raped would rip her virgin's apparel to let everyone know that she had been raped. This was to remove some of the humiliation from her and bring shame upon the man who'd raped her.

Why did Tamar put ashes on her head?

- This coupled with her ripped garment meant she had been "humbled". A virgin could walk about proud, but a woman who had become a wife through intercourse was considered "humbled". Ashes represented dust; thus saying that the person is acknowledging that they are made of dirt.

What does all of this have to do with you?

- The modern day church is like Tamar. Many of you have been deceived into practicing pagan rituals.
- You were once admired by the world, and you were seduced into doctrines that go against the living GOD.

- You were then raped and plundered; stripped of your holiness, and sent out to walk about the earth as a humiliated people.
- You come before the LORD with the scent of the gods of the world on you. Because of this, you have become a whoremonger.
- Even when you learn of your errors, you still refuse to repent; instead, you justify your ways and continue to lie with the gods of the Babylonians.

Understand this: JEHOVAH is GOD; therefore, HE has made HIMSELF one with the believer. Just as a wife carries the soul of her husband, a believer carries the SPIRIT of GOD. *"What? Know ye not that your body is the temple of the Holy Ghost which is in you, which ye have of God, and ye are not your own" (1 Corinthians 6:19)?* When you go about practicing paganism, you are doing so in the presence of GOD. When you send out that Valentine's Day card, you are worshipping Nimrod aka Osiris aka Tammuz. When you decorate those Easter eggs, you are in the same representing the pagan goddesses Ishtar and/or Ēostre. When you read your horoscope, you are in the same a representative of the worship of celestial beings.

The story for Tamar had a pretty decent ending, if we can call it that. Absalom avenged his sister and killed Amnon. After all, Absalom was the whole brother of Tamar; Amnon was her half brother. It was thought to have been done to get revenge against Amnon, but in reality, Absalom was redeeming his sister. If Amnon was dead, her shame would go away and she would be able to remarry and possibly have children someday. Absalom waited two years for Amnon to repent of what he'd done

275

and redeem Tamar, but he did not. Sadly enough, however, Absalom turned on his father, David, and was eventually killed.

CHRIST is better than Absalom

CHRIST redeemed us from the defiling we'd endured. HE gave HIS life and took the punishment for us so that we could be reconciled to our FATHER which is in Heaven. We are now free to be brides of CHRIST. Our robes are pure again; therefore, we don't have to rip them or be ashamed anymore. *"And I heard as it were the voice of a great multitude, and as the voice of many waters, and as the voice of mighty thunderings, saying, Alleluia: for the Lord God omnipotent reigneth.*
Let us be glad and rejoice, and give honour to him: for the marriage of the Lamb is come, and his wife hath made herself ready. And to her was granted that she should be arrayed in fine linen, clean and white: for the fine linen is the

righteousness of saints" (Revelation 19:6-8).

Come out of her, o ye Saints of GOD! This world's system is the great whore that rides upon the beast in the book of Revelation. It is the Babylonian system that still seduces America and other great nations into sexual immorality. Those who committed adultery with her are the believers (royalty of GOD.) *"So he carried me away in the spirit into the wilderness: and I saw a woman sit upon a scarlet coloured beast, full of* **names of blasphemy**, *having seven heads and ten horns. And the woman was arrayed in purple and scarlet colour, and decked with gold and precious stones and pearls, having a golden cup in her hand full of abominations and filthiness of her fornication: And upon her forehead was a name written, MYSTERY, BABYLON THE GREAT, THE MOTHER OF HARLOTS AND ABOMINATIONS OF THE*

*EARTH. And I saw the woman **drunken with the blood of the saints**, and with the **blood of the martyrs of Jesus**: and when I saw her, I wondered with great admiration" (Revelation 17:3-6).*

The system is a whore! Just as a married man could not justify lying with a woman who is not his wife, we cannot justify serving under a system of devil worship! Could a man tell his wife that he laid with the other woman, BUT he made it right by ministering to her before and after the act? Why do many believe this is acceptable to GOD? Why do many believe they can justify being ruled by this system, just as long as they say a few scriptures to a few people while under it?

Chapter 17

You are Not the World

I remember when I was in the second grade, and this song came out called *We are the World*. I absolutely adored that song, and I would sing it for years to come, until one day, I heard it from a different angle. I was no longer in the world, so I didn't like saying that I was the world. The lyrics to the song were powerful and somewhat true. We do need to pull together as one to change the earth (not the world); we do need to lend a helping hand, but how can we do this with the world? When we hear the term "world", we automatically think of the earth, but they are not one and the same. The earth is the ground we step on, and the planet we live on. The world is the system of man in the earth. Strong's Concordance Bible defines world as:

kosmos: order, the world

Original Word: κόσμος, ου, ὁ
Part of Speech: Noun, Masculine
Transliteration: kosmos
Phonetic Spelling: (kos'-mos)
Short Definition: the world, universe
Definition: the world, universe; worldly affairs; the inhabitants of the world; adornment.
Helps™ Word Studies says this of the word

"world": *kósmos (literally, "something ordered")*

– properly, an "ordered system" (like the universe, creation); the world.

[The English term "cosmetic" is derived from kósmos, i.e. the order ("ensemble") used of treating the face as a whole.]

Somehow, over the course of time, we have come to believe that earth and world are the

same. But why would GOD reject the earth
when HE created it? When GOD refers to the
world, HE is referring to the system or order of
this world. Here are some scriptures to help
you better understand the difference:

- **Genesis 1:2**- *"<u>And the earth</u> was
  without form, and void; and darkness
  was upon the face of the deep. And the
  Spirit of God moved upon the face of
  the waters."*

The earth was without form. This shows us
that GOD was creating the earth in which we
live.

- **Galatians 1:4**- *"Who gave himself for
  our sins, that he might deliver us from
  this present <u>evil world</u>, according to the
  will of God and our Father..."*

CHRIST delivered us from this evil world, not
the earth. If HE had delivered us from the
earth, we must ask ourselves: Why are we still
here? Did we miss HIM when HE saved the

elect? No, CHRIST delivered us from this world's system.

- **Romans 5:12**- *"Wherefore, as by one man <u>sin entered into the world</u>, and death by sin; and so death passed upon all men, for that all have sinned..."*

Through Adam, sin entered into the system of the world. The earth had already been created, and Satan was already walking about the earth; that's how he was able to deceive Eve and snare Adam. GOD created a system for man, and the system became the law of the world. Those who are under the law (unbelievers) are of the world, because they are in the world's system; therefore, they have subjected themselves to the law. The law isn't just the Mosaic-law since Moses hadn't yet come; the law was the commands that GOD gave to Adam and Eve and the curse that they fell under because of their sins. Every man that was born to Adam and Eve (their lineage) was born into sin because there was no redemption for sins at that time. Because of this, death was passed generation to generation, since GOD created us in HIS likeness. What this means is GOD created us to produce creatures or seeds after our own kind. When Adam and Eve sinned, their children were born as sinners.

- **2 Peter 3:5-7**- *"For this they willingly are ignorant of, that by the word of God the heavens were of old, <u>and the earth standing out of the water</u> and in the water: Whereby <u>the world that then was</u>, being overflowed with water, <u>perished</u>: But the heavens and the earth, which are now, by the same word are kept in store, reserved unto fire against the day of judgment and perdition of ungodly men."*

This is one of the clearest definitions yet since these scriptures contain both the term "earth" and the term "world". First, the term earth was used to explain the physical earth. It tells us that it was standing out on water and in water. The earth was covered with water. This is indeed referring to the great flood that destroyed all mankind except Moses and those who went aboard the ark with him. Then, the scriptures go on to tell us that the world perished. It was not referring to the earth that we live in, for this is still the same earth that Noah lived upon. Do you believe that GOD created another earth at that time, and caused Noah to sail over into that earth? No. The earth was not destroyed; the system of man in the earth, and everything that was in the earth, was destroyed. All living things were destroyed, but the Bible tells us that the water eventually subsided, and Noah and his family were able to leave the ark eventually.

When the flood came upon the earth, it was

sent to destroy mankind and his system, for the system was evil. Genesis 6:1-7 sheds more light on this topic:

*"And it came to pass, when men began to multiply on the **face of the earth**, and daughters were born unto them, That the sons of God saw the daughters of men that they were fair; and they took them wives of all which they chose. And the LORD said, My spirit shall not always strive with man, for that he also is flesh: yet his days shall be an hundred and twenty years. There were giants in the earth in those days; and also after that, when the sons of God came in unto the daughters of men, and they bare children to them, the same became mighty men which were of old, men of renown.*

*And GOD saw that the wickedness of man was great **in the earth**, and that every imagination of the thoughts of his heart was only evil continually. And <u>it repented the LORD that he</u>*

had **made man on the earth**, and it grieved him at his heart. And the LORD said, I will destroy **man** whom I have created **from the face of the earth**; both man, and beast, and the creeping thing, and the fowls of the air; for it repenteth me that I have made them." Again, from the scriptures above, you can see that GOD did not repent of making the earth; GOD repented of making man on the earth because man was wicked. The sons of GOD, of course, were fallen angels or demons. From their unions with the women in the earth, giants were born. How did these fallen angels (demons) get into the realm of the earth? Revelation 12:9 answers this question: _"And the great dragon was cast out, that old serpent, called the Devil, and Satan, which deceiveth the whole world: he was cast out into the earth, and his angels were cast out with him."_ Of course, these giants were wicked, and a new system was formed that was wicked. When the Bible says these sons of GOD took the sons of men as wives, it does not mean they had a wedding ceremony and lived together. It means that they laid together. How did this happen? Hebrews 13:2 wraps it up for us: *"Be not forgetful to entertain strangers: for thereby some have entertained angels unawares."* Angels do often come in the form of men in the earth realm. Angels are spirits and because of this, they need an earth suit to physically interact with people; therefore, many came in the form of men, and they took wives (or laid with women), and children were born to these unions. Needless to say, the children born of these unions were incredibly wicked. After all, their dads were fallen angels! GOD destroyed the system of man by destroying all of mankind.

"And be not conformed to this world: but be ye transformed by the renewing of your mind, that

287

*ye may prove what is that good, and
acceptable, and perfect, will of God" (Romans
12:2).* Merriam-Webster Dictionary defines
conform and transform this way:

Conform:

- to be similar to or the same as
  something

- to obey or agree with something

- to do what other people do : to behave
  in a way that is accepted by most
  people

Transform:

- to change in composition or structure
- to change the outward form or
  appearance of
- to change in character or condition

Remember when I said that we should not look
like the world, act like the world or think like the

world? I used tattoos as an example. To be conformed isn't just an inward change; it is an outward change, for whatever happens on the inside of you will eventually manifest outwardly. To be conformed is to behave in a way that is acceptable by most people. How bad off is the church today?! We should NOT be accepted by the world, but many churches are accepted because they are in no way different than the world! They have bowed down to a system that hates the living GOD! They have welcomed mindsets that go against the WORD of GOD! To be transformed is to be changed inwardly and outwardly. It is not just a change that needs to be heard; it is a change that has to be seen! You can't go against GOD and be for HIM. You have to choose whom you are serving. *"And if it seem evil unto you to serve the Lord, choose you this day whom ye will serve; whether the gods which your fathers served that were on the other side of the*

flood, *or the gods of the Amorites, in whose land ye dwell: but as for me and my house, we will serve the LORD" (Joshua 24:15).*

When CHRIST died and was resurrected, HE redeemed us from the curse of the law. HE redeemed us from the system of this wicked world. John 15:19 informs us, *"If ye were of the world, the world would love his own: but because ye are not of the world, but I have chosen you out of the world, therefore the world hateth you."* You are not to try to fit in or be loved by a world who hates your FATHER. How much of a dishonor it is for GOD to see you defend your natural father but refuse to defend your Heavenly FATHER. How dishonorable and hurtful it must be to see your own children befriend and walk with people who hate you. How much of a betrayal it has to be to see the children in which you have protected and loved join hands with forces who are against you! But many in the church will continue to interlink their souls with the souls of the damned. They will continue to hold hands and follow these souls to the gates of hell. Someone told them that they could still be a part of the system and get into Heaven. Someone didn't read the whole Bible. CHRIST revealed to us what HE would do with such a soul.

- **Revelation 3:16**- *"So then because thou art lukewarm, and neither cold nor hot, I will spue thee out of my mouth."*

- **Matthew 7:21-23**- *"Not every one that saith unto me, Lord, Lord, shall enter into the kingdom of heaven; but he that doeth the will of my Father which is in heaven. Many will say to me in that day, Lord, Lord, have we not prophesied in thy name? and in thy name have cast out devils? and in thy name done many wonderful works? And then will I*

profess unto them, I never knew you:
depart from me, ye that work iniquity."

Out of fear, many continue to be Ahab'ed by
the world, but look at what happened to Ahab.
You will either walk in faith with GOD or walk in
fear against HIM. You cannot create a mixture
of worldliness and holiness and expect to enter
into the Kingdom of Heaven. With CHRIST,
you are either hot or cold, and if you can't
make the decision as to which of these you
want to be; HE will make that decision for you
by renouncing you. HE will not include you
when you chose to exclude HIM. *"For*
whosoever shall be ashamed of me and of my
words, of him shall the Son of man be
ashamed, when he shall come in his own glory,
and in his Father's, and of the holy angels"
(Luke 9:26).

But what about those souls who have

conformed with the intent of transforming others? They have rejected CHRIST. How so? To be transformed is to be transformed in CHRIST; to be conformed is to accept the system or mindset of a man. GOD never asked you to go undercover as a saint looking like a sinner to win souls for the Kingdom. HE told you how to win them in Matthew 5:16. *"Let your light so shine before men, that they may see your good works, and glorify your Father which is in heaven."* CHRIST did not dress up like the world, nor did HE present HIMSELF in a worldly way trying to win souls. HE simply spoke the truth, and those who wanted HIM came to HIM; those who did not want HIM continued to reject HIM. We were called to follow HIM, and not the other way around!

- **John 12:26**- *"If any man serve me, let him follow me; and where I am, there shall also my servant be: if any man serve me, him will my Father honour."*

- **Matthew 10:38**- *"And he that taketh not his cross, and followeth after me, is not worthy of me."*

As you read the scriptures, you will find that CHRIST never conformed to the world, nor did HE follow after HIS Disciples. Instead, HE passed them by and simply said to them, *"Follow me."* They didn't have time to think about it; they didn't have time to speak to HIM about it. They simply got up and followed HIM. HE didn't become worldly trying to win souls for the Kingdom of GOD. HE simply extended an invitation to them, but those who would not come made the choice to stay behind. *"And Jesus answered and spake unto them again by parables, and said, The kingdom of heaven is like unto a certain king, which made a marriage for his son, And sent forth his servants to call them that were bidden to the wedding: and they would not come. Again, he sent forth other servants, saying, Tell them which are bidden, Behold, I have prepared my dinner: my oxen and my fatlings are killed, and all things are ready: come unto the marriage. But they made light of it, and went their ways, one to his farm, another to his merchandise..."* *(Matthew 22:1-5).* CHRIST invited you and me to follow HIM, but the world has extended an invitation to us as well. Oftentimes, people take the world's invitation and operate in the world and with the world as a saint. This is unacceptable to GOD. Many would argue the fact that CHRIST sat with tax collectors and publicans, but what is not mentioned is the fact that they were coming after or following JESUS. When we seek CHRIST, HE will not reject us. *"And it came to pass, that, as Jesus sat at meat in his house, many publicans and sinners sat also together with Jesus and his disciples: for there were many, and they followed him. And when the scribes and Pharisees saw him eat with publicans and sinners, they said unto his disciples, How is it that he eateth and drinketh with publicans and sinners? When Jesus heard it, he saith unto them, They that are whole have no need of the physician, but they that are sick: I came not to call the righteous, but sinners to repentance"* (Mark 2:15-17). There are people who want CHRIST, and they will come after HIM, and it's okay to sit with them and share CHRIST with them. What is not okay is to try and force CHRIST upon people who do not want HIM. It is not okay to sit and dine with sinners who have no desire to know HIM. In that, they are not coming after CHRIST; the saints are coming after them. In doing so, they put themselves in harm's way for CHRIST came to call the sinners **to** repentance. When someone wants CHRIST, they will be transformed day by day into HIS likeness. When a saint goes amongst sinners, his mission is to lead the sinners **to** repentance;

not to be led by them into sin. He is simply there to be a light for those who want to follow CHRIST. As a saint, you cannot cover up your light in hopes of winning souls for CHRIST. *"No man, when he hath lighted a candle, putteth it in a secret place, neither under a bushel, but on a candlestick, that they which come in may see the light" (Luke 11:33).*

Please remember that you are a spirit born in an earthly body, and you were born into the earth. You are in the midst of this world just as the wheat was in the midst of the tares. You are not of this world; therefore, you cannot put on their ways, nor are you to cover up your light trying to merge yourself with darkness. The angels will one day come and take away those who are sealed by CHRIST, and they will be taken to their forever homes in Heaven. The former earth will be no more, and a new earth and a new Heaven will be created for the believers. *"And I saw a new heaven and a new earth: for the first heaven and the first earth were passed away; and there was no more sea" (Revelation 21:1).* The former earth will be destroyed, and everyone not found in the Book of Life will be cast into the lake which burns with fire and brimstone, where the smoke of their torment will rise forever and ever. Let's face it; this is all scriptural, and it is true; therefore, we have to stop trying to be who we are not and ask the LORD to reveal to us who we really are.

The world's system is not for the believer, but there are many believers who are snared by it and all of its beauty. It is inviting; it is appealing, and it is hard to not want to join in and enjoy the pleasantries set forth by it. But it's also not worth it. The world's system is against GOD; therefore, as believers, we must be against the system so that we can be for

GOD. Does this mean that we need to strap up for war against the world? No way. We are simply to be a light so that those who want CHRIST will see our lights shining and will come follow after the CHRIST in us. We have to live amongst the world for this short time, but the struggle is to not become so charmed by this world that we decide to sample it and then end up addicted to it. You are not of this world; you are simply living in the midst of it. Remember, when you stand in CHRIST, the world will hate you. When you fall into sin, the world will love you. Either you are for GOD or you are against HIM. There is no in-between, and there will be no lukewarm saints who are "cool" enough to hang with the world and "hot" enough to charm their way into Heaven. *"No man can serve two masters: for either he will hate the one, and love the other; or else he will hold to the one, and despise the other. Ye cannot serve God and mammon" (Matthew*

6:24). GOD lives in the heart of the believer, but if you refuse to let HIM enter your heart to dwell there, why would HE allow you to live in Heaven? Think about it.

Chapter 18

Top Heavy, Bottom Fed

Every believer who wants to live a life pleasing to GOD must separate himself from this man-made system. We have to stop allowing ourselves to be enticed into temptation. When John had the vision in the Book of Revelation, he marveled after the whore who sat on the beast. He was then asked by the angel his reason for marveling after her. *"And I saw the woman drunken with the blood of the saints, and with the blood of the martyrs of Jesus: and when I saw her, I wondered with great admiration. And the angel said unto me,*

301

Wherefore didst thou marvel? I will tell thee the mystery of the woman, and of the beast that carrieth her, which hath the seven heads and ten horns" (Revelation 17:6-7).

As human beings, we are easily captivated by anything that has the appearance of beauty, wealth, power and mystery. This captivation has caused many saints to fall into temptation. This marveling has caused many who were the head to start operating as a tail.

One thing we must understand as the church is that the world's system hates GOD and all of HIS ways. Pay attention to how one of the world's greatest powers (America) is rapidly removing GOD from everything. People are literally being imprisoned for refusing to go against what GOD said. But the worst of it is yet to come. Right now, you will find that more than half of the Christian churches in establishment have linked themselves up with this world's system in one way or another. The system shows the church the benefits of becoming one with it, and many have fallen into this temptation. The system is referred to as Jezebel in the book of Revelation because the original Jezebel was given a position of authority over the people of GOD. This was a position she was NOT supposed to have. Now, the world's system is positioning itself over the church by accepting every religious belief as one equal to the gospel of JESUS CHRIST. Because of this, leaders are more determined to be "fair-minded" towards cults and every belief under the sun for the sake of pacifying an increasingly wicked nation. The world's system is now a system of Baal worship and paganism.

Dearest believer; you are not of this world, nor should you be for it. This system is becoming more and more top heavy as the love of money continues to advance into the hearts of those who are under it. Anyone who is under this system will continue to fold under its pressure as man continues to try to replace GOD with governmental rule. Anyone under the system will be the legs of the system, carrying around the weight of those who are at the top. Man can't replace GOD, and his attempts will prove to be vain. What you are seeing in this 21st century is not new. Thousands of years ago, this very same system was established and brought down to its knees, forced to acknowledge that JESUS CHRIST is LORD. There were pagans amongst believers back then, and GOD was and continues to be faithful to HIS elect. In the days of Moses, GOD parted the Red Sea to let HIS people cross over, and HE tossed the sea back upon the Egyptians who were pursuing them. When Jezebel ruled, GOD gave her time to repent, but after a while, HE sent Jehu to dethrone her and every child born of her forever. Many of HIS Prophets fell under her sword, but hell cannot claim their souls. Certain Jews released a murderer so they could crucify JESUS, but they had no idea that they were being used to fulfill a prophesy. Even after they crucified HIM, HE still arose, and HE lives forevermore. Death could not hold HIM, and hell could not retain HIM. HE lives! What about you? Are you going to let a man-made system take HIS seat in your heart? Are you going to let the love of money (spirit of mammon) cause you to fall under judgment? This system is not for you, no matter how much you see the benefits of serving under it. This system is against your FATHER; therefore, this system is against you.

Believers who find themselves under the world's system will find that they are the least in the system. They will be the crud of the system; the Lazarus sitting at the gates of a wicked man's house hoping to snag a crumb. They will be forced to choose between GOD and Mammon, and many of them will choose the wicked spirit of Mammon. Mammon is the spirit that seduces people into loving money. Just like those who are in the world, they will begin to refer to Mammon as god, not understanding that JEHOVAH is GOD. They will justify their ways and even misquote scriptures to mislead others. They will forfeit their right to be called a Christian as they merge with the world and find themselves a part of a system that hates them. They will become slaves to a system who will in return use them to capture more slaves and slaughter anyone who refuses to get the mark of the beast. They will hate everyone who truly loves the LORD, and they will wrongfully judge anyone who does not follow after the god they are serving. In their left hands, you will find weapons designed to kill the elect of GOD. In their right hands or on their foreheads, you will find the mark of the beast. They will become prophets of Baal, coming out in numbers to prophesy against anyone who will not serve Jezebel. They will seek to slaughter the men and women after GOD'S own heart, but GOD will send a lying spirit amongst them to cause the Ahabs (church who went under their leadership) to fall. GOD will cast Jezebel from her wall once again, as HE sends out the Jehus and Elijahs to cut down the lineage of such a wicked system. Those who once claimed to love Jezebel will cast her down. They will be eunuchs; castrated and emasculated, and they will use the last of their strength to cast her down. The beast that she serves will be brought down to perdition, and everyone not found in the Book of Life will follow his lead. Many will come before the

LORD seeking entrance into Heaven, but they will be turned away as the mark of the beast is revealed on them. Many of them will be men and women of GOD who did many signs and wonders, not understanding that their powers were not derived from GOD; they were powers of darkness, or better yet, witchcraft. They chose to live under a system that was redesigned by the enemy to promote his agenda, and they will be swallowed whole into the fiery pit. The Truth is, was and is to come; therefore, those who open their hearts to receive HIM (the Truth) will receive HIM. Those who continue to fall after lies (Satan's doctrine) will become followers of Satan.

Truth is- *"Jesus saith unto him, I am the way, the **truth**, and the life: no man cometh unto the Father, but by me" (John 14:6).*

Word is- *"In the beginning was the **Word**, and the **Word** was with God, and the* **Word was God***. He was with God in the beginning.*

Through him all things were made; without him nothing was made that has been made. In him was life, and that life was the light of all mankind. The light shines in the darkness, and the darkness has not overcome it" (John 1:1-5).

JESUS light the way- *"Then spoke Jesus again unto them, saying, I am the **light of the world**: he that follows me shall not walk in darkness, but shall have the light of life" (John 8:12).*

JESUS is the way- *"Jesus saith unto him, **I am the way**, the truth, and the life: no man cometh unto the Father, but by me" (John 14:6).*

Satan is a liar- *"Ye are of your father the devil, and the lusts of your father ye will do. He was a murderer from the beginning, and abode not in the truth, because there is no truth in him. When he speaketh a lie, he speaketh of his own: **for he is a liar**, and the father of it" (John*

8:44).

JESUS is the light of the world. Satan is the darkness that covers the world. You cannot serve both GOD and Satan. *"No man can serve two masters: for either he will hate the one, and love the other; or else he will hold to the one, and despise the other. Ye cannot serve God and mammon" (Matthew 6:24).* Anytime you see a believer who is in the world, they will defend the world with everything in them, but they will not defend the WORD of GOD. Instead, they will oftentimes misquote the WORD to stand with the world. That's because they have chosen their master, and when they battle with the Truth, they are not battling against the one who spoke the Truth; they are battling against the Truth, HIMSELF. *"For we wrestle not against flesh and blood, but against principalities, against powers, against the rulers of the darkness of this world,*

*against spiritual wickedness in high places"
(Ephesians 6:12).* Again, JESUS is the living
WORD of GOD; HE is the Truth! That's why
GOD told us not to argue with them. You are
simply vessels of GOD; temples of the HOLY
SPIRIT who carry around the Truth in your
heart. You bring the Truth to those who want to
follow HIM, and they will decide if they want to
follow HIM or not. But in arguing with someone
who does not want HIM, you actually advance
the kingdom of darkness.

- **Proverbs 23:9**- *"Speak not in the ears
  of a fool: for he will despise the wisdom
  of thy words."*

- **Proverbs 26:4**- *"Answer not a fool
  according to his folly, lest thou also be
  like unto him."*

- **2 Timothy 2:14**- *"Of these things put
  them in remembrance, charging them
  before the Lord that they strive not
  about words to no profit, but to the*

311

subverting of the hearers."

Separate yourselves and be holy. *"Be ye not unequally yoked together with unbelievers: for what fellowship hath righteousness with unrighteousness? And what communion hath light with darkness" (2 Corinthians 6:14)?* Don't bow down to right-sounding wrongs. Get to know the LORD for yourself, so you won't be ensnared by the various doctrines that are going about the world right now. Again, remember, any believer under the system will eat the leftovers that are kicked out of the system, because a believer is elevated when he is in the WORD but demoted when he is in the world. You are not a serf, a vagabond or a peasant; you are royalty! Do whatever GOD has been telling you to do so you won't be wrapped up in this world's system when its legs give and those who trusted it can no longer hold it up. Believe it or not, the first ones who will fall under the system will be believers who have gone under it. The world loves its own, but it hates anyone who radiates holiness. Those who refer to themselves as Christians will be bottom-fed; given only what is left after the world has had its fill. They will work the hardest to hold up the unbelievers, defend their doctrines and fight against the uncompromising WORD of GOD. They will give off the appearance of holiness without the presence of holiness, and they will suffer the plagues reserved for the unbelievers because they too have turned away from the Truth to follow the doctrines of devils. *"For when they speak great swelling words of vanity, they allure through the lusts of the flesh, through much wantonness, those that were clean escaped from them who live in error. While they promise them liberty, they themselves are the servants of corruption: for of whom a man is overcome, of the same is he brought in bondage. For if after they have escaped the pollutions of the world through the knowledge of the Lord and Saviour Jesus Christ, they are again entangled therein, and overcome, the latter end is worse with them than the beginning. For it had been better for them not to have known the way of righteousness, than, after they have known it, to turn from the holy commandment delivered unto them. But it is happened unto them according to the true proverb, The dog is turned to his own vomit again; and the sow that was washed to her wallowing in the mire" (2 Peter 2:18-22).*

Remember, in CHRIST, you are the head of the world and you will come behind in no good thing. In the world, you are the tail of the system, and you will stay back there until they figure out what to do with you. The world's system is not for you or me; it is for those who are in the world. The original system was GOD-designed for man to simply rest and trust in HIM. CHRIST gave us that rest back, but we still have to endure the temptations and evil for just a little while. CHRIST is your head; stay in HIM as the body of CHRIST. That way, you will be led by HIM, and you can rest in the promises of GOD. Know this: The dead is told to rest in peace, but those who trust in GOD shall live in peace and rest in peace while they are still yet alive!

Here are a few things you should consider for your life:

1. You are royalty; therefore, you should live as such. You can only inherit your crown when you are in GOD'S will for your life. If you are off somewhere doing Satan's bidding, you'll inherit what GOD left for him.

2. The world can never give you what GOD has in store for you. Don't depend on man or his system; put your faith in

GOD only.

3. The world is like a microwave; it feeds the impatient. GOD is like an oven; if you will only wait on HIM, when your blessing is ready, it'll be worth the wait seven times over!

4. If you are on welfare, it's okay...just don't stay there. Make plans and a schedule to walk in your wealthy place.

5. Don't fear success! Most people who fear success don't know it until they are threatened with it. Bind up the spirit of fear, because fear is a form of reverence. When you fear GOD, you reverence HIM; when you fear anything other than GOD, you reverence it, thus making it an idol.

6. You are the head; stop acting like a tail. Don't wag every time the world throws you a crumb. Get up and get what belongs to you.

7. Ask GOD to change your relationship with money, food and everything that has shaped your walk in HIM. Ask HIM to give you a godly relationship with things and people, and you will begin to see the blessings coming after you.

8. In CHRIST, you are royalty; in the world, you're nothing more than a religious vagabond. Don't exchange your royalty for rags.

9. Your body can have several symptoms of illness, but if your mouth has one WORD from GOD, and you believe that WORD, you can cause sickness and disease to bow down and declare that JESUS CHRIST is LORD. In doing so, you will cause sickness and disease to honor HIS WORD for the believer and get their hands off you.

10. The system was originally designed for the people of GOD, but it has been

perverted; therefore, CHRIST came and saved us from it. Don't go back under it!

11. The government practices what is best referred to as "religious tolerance". They will tolerate you, but the system is not designed to favor you. You will begin to see more rights given to anti-CHRIST religions than Christians because of the growing prejudice against Christianity.

12. Believers will continue to be weighed down by mounting debt. This is a way to keep you entangled up in this world's system and cause you to serve as a slave to it.

13. Believers who stay under the system will be forced to oppose believers who refuse to submit to it. They will depend on the system, believe in the system, and kill for the system. Like Jehoshaphat, they will be sent into wars

wearing their royal garments. They will be too blind to recognize that they are worthless targets to a system that sees them as disposable.

14. The top will continue to get heavier as mainstream media is now glorifying ignorance, demonic behaviors, murder, adultery and everything ungodly. You do not want to be standing under this system when it buckles.

Paganism is beginning to crawl back to the top of the religious pyramid. The best position for you, as a believer, is to stay in CHRIST and denounce everything unlike GOD. Denounce the pagan practices of this nation, and don't ever allow those devils into your home anymore. In doing so, you will reap the benefits of your faithfulness. It may seem hard at first, because we have all grown accustomed to this world's system. Just as it is not easy to divorce a person whom you have grown to love and feel comfortable with, it is not easy to divorce a way of thinking and living that you have come to love and feel comfortable with. Nevertheless, it can be done, it should be done, and it has to be done. We are the very elect of GOD; we come behind in no good thing! You can never get your inheritance if you are acting as a child of Satan. The inheritance of GOD was left for HIS people who are operating as HIS sons and daughters, without shame or fear. With CHRIST as the head of your life, you will never be weighed down with the cares of this world. *"Cast your burden upon the LORD, and he shall sustain you: he shall never permit the righteous to be moved" (Psalm 55:22).*

Don't be standing on the wrong side of wrong when CHRIST comes back to judge the earth. After all, GOD gets the last word in all of this.

"I am Alpha and Omega, the beginning and the ending, saith the Lord, which is, and which was, and which is to come, the Almighty" (Revelation 1:8).